USS
JOHN F. KENNEDY

in detail & scale

Bert Kinzey

KALMBACH BOOKS

Airlife Publishing Ltd.
England

Copyright 1993 by Detail & Scale, Inc. All rights reserved. This book may not be reproduced in part or in whole without written permission from the publisher, except in the case of brief quotations used in reviews. Published by Kalmach Publishing Company, 21027 Crossroads Circle, P.O. Box 1612, Waukesha, Wisconsin 53187.

CONTRIBUTORS AND SOURCES:

Dana Bell
USS JOHN F. KENNEDY, CV-67
COMNAVAIRLANT Public Affairs Office

U.S. Navy
Department of Defense
National Archives

The author thanks LCDR Steve Honda of the COMNAVAIRLANT Public Affairs Office and his former assistant, LTJG Robert Mehal, for their assistance in arranging a visit to the USS JOHN F. KENNEDY for the purpose of taking photographs and doing research.

A special word of thanks goes to LT Terry Evans, the KENNEDY's Public Affairs Officer at the time this book was researched. LT Evans filled every possible request by providing information and access for photographic opportunities. The author sincerely appreciates his assistance and cooperation.

Many photographs in this book are credited to their contributors. Photographs with no credit indicated were taken by the author.

Library of Congress Cataloging-in-Publication Data

Kinzey, Bert.
 The USS John F. Kennedy : in detail & scale / by Bert Kinzey
  p. cm. -- (D. & S. ; v. 42)
 ISBN 0-89024-173-2180-5 : $11.95
 1. Enterprise (Aircraft carrier :
  CVA (N) 67)   I. Title.
[VA65.J5K56 1993]
623.8'255--dc20
             93-1022
              CIP

First published in Great Britain in 1993
by Airlife Publishing, Ltd.
7 St. John's Hill, Shrewsbury, SY1 1JE

British Library Cataloguing in Publication Data
 A catalogue record for this book
 is available from the British library

ISBN: 1 85310 639 9

Front cover: *The USS JOHN F. KENNEDY, CV-67, operates in the Red Sea during Operation Desert Storm. Aircraft of Carrier Air Wing Three can be seen on her flight deck, and these include the last two A-7E Corsair II squadrons in U.S. Navy service.*
(USS JOHN F. KENNEDY)

Rear cover: *The layout of KENNEDY's huge 4.56-acre flight deck is clearly illustrated in this photograph that was taken from high overhead. A Tomcat is spotted on cat three, while an Intruder is on cat four. The ready helicopter is positioned well forward in the landing area and will take off for plane guard duties before air operations begin. Fifty-eight aircraft of all types in the air wing can be seen on the flight deck, while the rest of Carrier Air Wing Three is below on the hangar deck.* *(USS JOHN F. KENNEDY)*

INTRODUCTION

This head-on view of KENNEDY was taken in the mid-seventies, and shows the ship in her earlier configuration. Note that there are two catapult overruns on the bow, and that the superstructure is solid gray. The forward, port, and aft faces of the lower superstructure have since been painted black. The 67 on the flight deck is solid white instead of being the white outline it is today. **(National Archives)**

This is the forty-second title in the Detail & Scale Series of aviation publications and the fifth about one of the aircraft carriers in the U.S. Navy. Previously we have done books on the USS LEXINGTON, USS AMERICA, USS FORRESTAL, and the nuclear powered USS ENTERPRISE. Each of these carriers was in a different class, and now we turn our attention to the USS JOHN F. KENNEDY, CV-67, which belongs to yet another unique one-ship class. As the last conventionally powered aircraft carrier built for the U.S. Navy, KENNEDY shares design features with the KITTY HAWK class which came before her, and the nuclear powered NIMITZ class which came later. All of these features are covered with detailed photography on the pages that follow.

In each of our previous books on aircraft carriers we have had a different area of emphasis in the section about the ship's operational service. With the USS LEXINGTON we focused on that ship's historical record that dates back to the great carrier battles of World War II. In the book about the USS AMERICA, we discussed the rigorous training, qualifying, maintenance, and deployment schedules followed by the Navy's carriers. Because FORRESTAL was the first super carrier, the emphasis was on the design considerations that went into that ship as opposed to the carriers that came before her. ENTERPRISE was the first nuclear powered carrier, so it was appropriate to examine the various aspects of using nuclear power in aircraft carriers. With KENNEDY, we will look at how a modern carrier uses her striking power as an instrument of U.S. policy in regional warfare which seems to be so prevalent today. This is done by providing a detailed account of KENNEDY's participation in Operation Desert Storm. After a brief summary of the ship's history, which covers the time period that begins with the laying of its keel on October 22, 1964, and ends on August 1, 1990, the KENNEDY's participation in the Gulf War is explained in considerable detail. This will help the reader understand just how an aircraft carrier is employed to play an important role during a conflict in which the United States may become involved.

Carrier Air Wing Three is also covered in this book. Aircraft from each squadron are illustrated, and the markings used by each are shown in general and close-up photographs. But as always the main emphasis of the publication is on the many physical details of the KENNEDY. Historical photographs, when compared to those taken more recently, show changes made to the ship over the years. Every major area from stem to stern and from the mast to the rudders is illustrated and described in detail. We have included scores of photographs that show the radars, catapults, arresting gear, elevators, flight deck details, the hangar bays, weapons systems, superstructure, bridges, pri-fly, and much more.

While many of the photographs in this book came from the National Archives, the Department of Defense Still Media Records Center, and the photo section of the KENNEDY herself, many more were taken specifically for this publication by the author and the noted aviation author and researcher, Dana Bell. Both of them flew out to the ship while she was conducting operations off the Atlantic coast in April 1992, and between them they took over 2,000 photographs. From these, the photos in this book were chosen to illustrate every possible detail of the carrier.

Concluding this book is a modelers section that explains how to take the two existing model kits of the USS JOHN F. KENNEDY and build them to represent the ship in her earlier configuration or as she appears today.

This book would not have been possible without the assistance of several people. Two of them deserve recognition here. LTJG Bob Mehal, formerly of the COMNAVAIRLANT Public Affairs Office, did the legwork that made the trip out to the KENNEDY possible. LT Terry Evans, the public affairs officer aboard KENNEDY at the time Dana Bell and the author visited the ship, made everything happen. He set up two flights in helicopters for the purpose of taking general and detailed photographs, and he arranged for access to the flight deck during air operations. He also coordinated the photography in the various spaces within the ship and provided a considerable amount of information about the carrier and her role in Operations Desert Shield and Desert Storm. To both of these gentlemen, the author expresses a sincere word of thanks.

SHIP'S HISTORY
EARLY HISTORY

In the early 1950s, the Korean conflict convinced American military planners that future armed confrontations did not necessarily have to take the form of all-out nuclear warfare. In fact, there was a considerably greater possibility that the United States would find itself involved in limited wars like the one in Korea. These brushfire wars were regional in scope, meaning that they could flare up almost anywhere on the globe where American interest were involved, but where there may not be adequate land bases in the vicinity.

The war in Korea also cast the deciding vote in the debate that had questioned the viability of the aircraft carrier, and it reversed the anti-carrier sentiment that had caused the cancellation of the super carrier USS UNITED STATES in 1949. Upon the outbreak of hostilities in Korea, funds were made available to activate more aircraft carriers in the U.S. Navy. Modernization programs were put into effect, and plans to build the first class of super carriers were begun in earnest.

Also contributing to the renewed interest in aircraft carriers was the fact that nuclear weapons were being made smaller and lighter so that they could be carried on fighter and attack aircraft. This meant that carrier based aircraft could be used to deliver nuclear weapons. The idea of basing part of America's nuclear deterrence on mobile bases at sea rather than having them on fixed land bases helped increase the all important survivability factor for part of this nuclear striking force.

New design features, most notably the angled landing area and the steam catapult, insured that high performance aircraft could be operated from aircraft carriers and silenced the critics who had claimed that the restrictions of carrier operations would mean that land based aircraft would be superior to those which had to take off and land aboard ships.

By 1954 it was evident that aircraft carriers could play vital roles in limited warfare and also be an important part of America's nuclear deterrence capability. They could be used to project power almost anywhere it was needed, and every U.S. President since the end of World War II has sent aircraft carriers to trouble spots around the globe in response to deteriorating political and/or military situations.

Because of these factors, the Eisenhower Administration began an ambitious program to significantly increase the carrier forces in the United States Navy. Existing carriers, many of which had been in mothballs since the end of World War II, were modernized so that they could operate jet aircraft. New electronic systems were added as were angled decks, stronger catapults, and improved arresting gear. ESSEX class carriers that had fought the great carrier battles against the Japanese in the Pacific rejoined the Navy, but their appearance had been altered considerably. The three ships of the newer MIDWAY class likewise received modernizations.

More importantly, part of the effort to increase the Navy's carrier forces was a new shipbuilding program that began with the construction of the first super carrier, USS FORRESTAL, CVA-59, in 1954. The Eisenhower Administration wanted one new super carrier to join the fleet each year, and they maintained this schedule until the Kennedy Administration took over in 1961. FORRESTAL was commissioned in 1955, and was followed by SARATOGA in 1956, RANGER in 1957, and INDEPENDENCE in early 1959. KITTY HAWK, CONSTELLATION, and the nuclear powered ENTERPRISE were launched in 1960, and they were all commissioned in 1961.

The new Kennedy Administration reopened questions about the value of aircraft carriers, and one of President Kennedy's "whiz kids," Secretary of Defense Robert Strange McNamara began an examination of carriers as well as other weapon systems. The keel for the USS AMERICA, CVA-66, had been laid on January 9, 1961, just two weeks before President Kennedy took office, but it did not join the Navy as a commissioned ship until 1965. Meanwhile, the Kennedy Administration halted the construction of new carriers for over three and a half years while McNamara argued with the admirals about aircraft carriers.

McNamara did not believe that the Navy needed another large carrier, so the keel laying for the next carrier was postponed. If a new carrier was to be built at all, McNamara contended that it should be conventionally powered. He argued that the initial costs of a nuclear powered carrier were too high. However, the Navy, which had by this time gained significant experience with nuclear powered surface ships, to include the carrier ENTERPRISE and the cruiser LONG BEACH, argued that the many operational advantages of nuclear power were well worth the cost. Additionally, the fact that the carrier would not

The keel for CV-67 was laid on October 22, 1964, eleven months after President John F. Kennedy was assassinated in Dallas, Texas. The sign on the building way at left indicates that the carrier was hull number 577 at the Newport News Shipbuilding and Drydock Company. At right is the plate that is displayed on the quarterdeck of the carrier. At the bottom of this plate is a quote from the late president that states, "Let every nation know that we shall pay any price, bear any burden, support any friend or oppose any foe, to assure the survival and success of liberty." With the wholesale cutbacks in defense spending in today's very unstable world, one must wonder if President Kennedy's own political party has forgotten this message. (Left National Archives, right author)

This is the KENNEDY's keel on the building way at the Newport News Shipbuilding and Drydock Company. KENNEDY was the last conventionally powered aircraft carrier built for the U.S. Navy.
(National Archives)

burn millions of gallons of fuel oil over its expected life span made the long term costs more attractive.

President Kennedy's term in office ended on November 22, 1963, when he was shot in Dallas, Texas. During his entire time as President, the argument between his Secretary of Defense and the Navy had continued, and not one keel had been laid for a new aircraft carrier. Mr. McNamara continued as Secretary of Defense under President Lyndon Johnson, and as the potential for conflict in Vietnam increased, Congress agreed to fund construction for a new carrier. However, McNamara remained steadfast in his position that the ship would be conventionally powered. This proved to be one of many short-sighted decisions made by Mr. McNamara due to his lack of a technical understanding of military systems and hardware. With the rising price of oil, the long term economic advantages of providing CVA-67 with nuclear power are obvious as they should have been in 1964. Further, her operational capabilities would have been significantly increased through the use of nuclear power. Fortunately, Mr. McNamara's ill-advised decision only effected one carrier, and all U.S. aircraft carriers built after the USS JOHN F. KENNEDY are in the nuclear powered NIMITZ class.

The circumstances that resulted in CVA-67 being named the USS JOHN F. KENNEDY are indeed both interesting and curious. Had the start of construction for this carrier not been delayed while the Secretary of Defense and the Navy argued over the use of nuclear power, the ship would not have been named for President Kennedy. This is because the keel would have been laid, and the carrier would have been named before President Kennedy was assassinated in November 1963. Obviously, if the name for the ship had been selected prior to President Kennedy's death, some other name would have been chosen, because no carrier would be named for a President who

These two photographs show construction of the KENNEDY in progress. At left is a view from the bow looking aft, while the photo at right looks forward from the stern.
(Both National Archives)

President Kennedy's widow and children were on hand at the christening ceremonies and launching. The President's daughter, Caroline, christened the ship. Other members of the Kennedy family, Secretary of Defense Robert S. McNamara, and other Navy and civilian dignitaries can be seen in this photograph taken at christening ceremonies.
(USS JOHN F. KENNEDY)

The KENNEDY was launched on May 27, 1967, and moved to a drydock to be completed. Note how high the ship is sitting in the water as tugs begin to move her to the drydock. Long sheds cover the four catapult tracks, and the superstructure is still surrounded with scaffolding. *(National Archives)*

was in office at the time it was built. It therefore seems ironic that the only carrier affected by McNamara's decision to use conventional power is now named for the President who selected him to be Secretary of Defense.

The keel for CVA-67 was finally laid on October 22, 1964, at the Newport News Shipbuilding and Drydock Company. She was christened by the late President's nine-year-old daughter, Caroline, and launched on May 27, 1967. She joined the Navy as a commissioned ship on September 7, 1968. Although she was similar to the design of the KITTY HAWK class, KENNEDY was different enough to be considered a one-ship class. The forward part of her angled landing area had been widened and cut off at an angle. Other changes were made around her hull that permitted higher speeds in rough seas. But KENNEDY's most recognizable and distinguishing feature was her unique slanted smokestack which was angled to starboard in an attempt to divert gasses away from aircraft as they approach the carrier for landing.

KENNEDY was also built without the long range Terrier surface-to-air missile armament that was installed in the KITTY HAWK class. Although she was initially unarmed, KENNEDY was soon fitted with the short range Basic Point Defense Missile System (BPDMS) with the original version of the Sea Sparrow missile. Except for the fact that she is conventionally powered and therefore has a smokestack, many of KENNEDY's features are more like those of the subsequent NIMITZ class than the previous KITTY HAWK class.

Original plans called for KENNEDY to be fitted with an SQS-23 sonar system housed in the bow dome. This necessitated the use of a stem anchor on a hawsepipe, but the sonar system was not fitted. Of her four catapults, cats one, two, and four are C 13 steam catapults, each of which are 250 feet long. Catapult number three is a C 13, Mod 1, which is 310 feet long, and it permits even the heaviest aircraft to be launched when the ship is at anchor with no wind over the deck. The 250-foot long standard C 13 can launch a 78,000 pound aircraft at 160 miles per hour, and it can be fired once every sixty seconds.

After the normal shakedown cruise, KENNEDY joined the

These two photographs show the KENNEDY as she put to sea for builder's trials. As originally completed, she carried no defensive armament. however, the three sponsons that would later mount launchers for the Basic Point Defense Missile System (BPDMS) can be seen in these views. *(Both National Archives)*

A starboard view shows KENNEDY shortly after entering service with the U.S. Navy. Mk 25 BPDMS launchers are now in place on their sponsons. (National Archives)

Atlantic Fleet, and through the early 1970s she made several deployments to the Mediterranean Sea. She also operated in the North Atlantic as well. During 1973 and 1974, she underwent modifications to permit replacement of the F-4 Phantom with the F-14 Tomcat in her air wing. At the same time, the capability to operate the S-3A Viking anti-submarine warfare aircraft was also added as part of the Navy's "CV concept." This was necessitated by the retirement of aging ESSEX class CVS anti-submarine warfare support carriers. Since the ESSEX class carriers were not replaced with new ASW carriers, the former attack carriers had to perform both the attack and ASW missions. This meant that the ability to operate ASW aircraft had to be added to each carrier. All but two former attack carriers were modified under this "CV concept," and the A was dropped from their designations. KENNEDY thus became CV-67 instead of CVA-67. The two carriers that were not modified under this concept were the USS MIDWAY, and the USS CORAL SEA. Neither of these two older carriers could operate the F-14 or the S-3A, mainly because of the low overhead clearance of their hangar bays. As a result, they both continued to operate F-4 Phantoms in the fighter squadrons of their air wings until they were replaced by F/A-18 Hornets. Neither ever operated the S-3 Viking.

By 1978, KENNEDY was ten years old and ready for a major overhaul. After a yard period that lasted one year, she began a series of workups, operational evaluations, and qualifications. KENNEDY's ninth deployment was made in 1981, and it was her first to the Indian Ocean. During that deployment, she recorded her 150,000th arrested landing.

In 1983, the growing crisis in Beirut, Lebanon, caused the United States to increase its military presence in that part of the world. KENNEDY was called upon to be a part of this presence, and it was at this time that she participated in combat for the first time when aircraft from her air wing flew strikes against targets in Lebanon. On December 3, 1983, KENNEDY was in the news when one of her A-6E Intruders was shot down over Lebanon. The A-6E was piloted by LT Mark Lange, and the bombardier/

During the night of November 22, 1975, the KENNEDY was involved in a collision with the USS BELKNAP, CG-26, while the ships operated in the Mediterranean Sea near Sicily. Almost the entire superstructure of the BELKNAP was destroyed, as shown in this photograph. However, the cruiser was repaired and put back in service.
(National Archives)

Damage to the KENNEDY was severe, but far less than that received by the BELKNAP. This view shows damage to the port side overhang where the cruiser struck the carrier. (National Archives)

Several types of aircraft that were in KENNEDY's first air wing are illustrated on this page. At left, an RA-5C Vigilante is moved on to one of the bow catapults for launching. Under its nose, a Skywarrior and two A-4 Skyhawks are visible, while under the aircraft's center section, the nose of an F-4B Phantom can be seen. In the background is an E-1B Tracer early warning aircraft. At right, an A-1 Skyraider is positioned on catapult number one. RA-5C Vigilantes can be seen to the left in the photograph, while an E-1B Tracer moves up toward the catapult from the right. In her early operational life, KENNEDY had to carry both jet fuel and AVGAS for her air wing.
(Both National Archives)

An A-4 Skyhawk catches the wire as it makes an arrested recovery aboard the KENNEDY. This photograph also shows details of the early configuration for the superstructure to include the carrier's unique slanted smokestack. Note that the lower section of the island is not painted black as it is today.
(National Archives)

The KENNEDY refuels the destroyer USS ALLEN M. SUMMNER, DD-692, in 1972. The SUMMNER was a World War II destroyer that was built in 1943, and she was the lead ship for the SUMMNER class. Many World War II destroyers served well into the 1970s and beyond, because insufficient funds were available in the defense budget to build an adequate number of new ships. This photograph dramatically illustrates the size comparison between the two ships.
(National Archives)

navigator was LT Robert Goodman. LT Lange was killed, but LT Goodman was captured and held prisoner for over a month before being returned to the United States. (LT Goodman's own personal account of his ordeal can be found in Detail & Scale Volume 24 on the A-6 Intruder.)

In July 1986, KENNEDY was in the news again, but this time it was for an entirely different reason. She was the centerpiece for a vast naval armada during the International Naval Review in honor of the 100th Anniversary/Rededication of the Statue of Liberty. President Reagan addressed the nation from her flight deck on the Fourth of July just before the start of the huge fireworks spectacular around the Statue of Liberty. The next month KENNEDY departed for a deployment to the Mediterranean that lasted until the following March.

Her twelfth major deployment to the Mediterranean began in August 1988. On January 4, 1989, while conducting routine operations in international waters, F-14s from the KENNEDY shot down two Libyan MiG-23 Floggers that were approaching the battle group in a hostile manner. This action was not unlike a similar incident in August 1981 when F-14s from the USS NIMITZ shot down two Libyan Su-22s. The result was the same in both cases. Two Libyan aircraft were destroyed without loss or damage to U.S. aircraft. For two years following this action against enemy aircraft, life for the KENNEDY and her air wing was hectic but routine. After visiting New York City for Fleet Week '90 and Boston for a Fourth of July visit, KENNEDY tied up at her pier at the Norfolk Navy Base. No one then knew how dramatically things would change the following month.

On July 4, 1986, President Reagan addressed the nation from the flight deck of the KENNEDY as the ship took part in the International Naval Review celebrating the centennial of the Statue of Liberty.
(Official U.S. Navy Photograph by PH1 R. E. Kerns)

OPERATION DESERT STORM

The USS JOHN F. KENNEDY rests at its pier at the Norfolk Navy Base on August 1, 1990. This was the day that Iraq invaded Kuwait. Just two weeks later, the carrier and her air wing left Norfolk for an emergency deployment in support of Operations Desert Shield and Desert Storm. This photograph was taken by the author from the superstructure of the USS ENTERPRISE, CVN-65, while he was shooting photographs for a book on that ship. (See Detail & Scale Volume 39.)

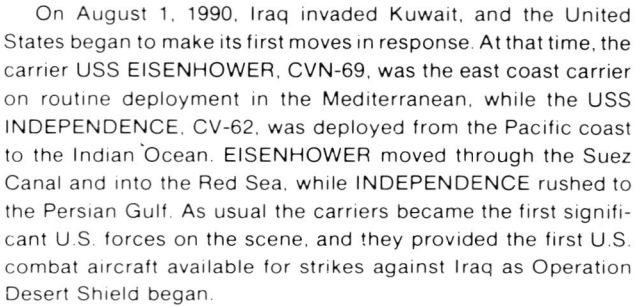

The KENNEDY transits the Suez Canal as part of the U.S. Naval force that participated in Operation Desert Storm. She was one of six carriers that launched strikes during the Gulf War.
(Official U.S. Navy Photograph)

On August 1, 1990, Iraq invaded Kuwait, and the United States began to make its first moves in response. At that time, the carrier USS EISENHOWER, CVN-69, was the east coast carrier on routine deployment in the Mediterranean, while the USS INDEPENDENCE, CV-62, was deployed from the Pacific coast to the Indian Ocean. EISENHOWER moved through the Suez Canal and into the Red Sea, while INDEPENDENCE rushed to the Persian Gulf. As usual the carriers became the first significant U.S. forces on the scene, and they provided the first U.S. combat aircraft available for strikes against Iraq as Operation Desert Shield began.

It was immediately clear that these two carriers would not be sufficient to respond to the threat posed by Iraq. The enormous amount of men and material moved into Kuwait by Iraq indicated a clear possibility that Iraq intended to invade Saudi Arabia next. Further, the EISENHOWER and INDEPENDENCE were both nearing the time that they were supposed to rotate home from their deployments. Six other carriers were quickly ordered to the Middle East, and KENNEDY was among them. Only four days after receiving orders, KENNEDY departed Norfolk on August 15, 1990. Carrier Air Wing Three flew out to the ship, and she headed for the Middle East. Among the units in CVW-3 were the last two squadrons to operate the A-7E Corsair II in Navy service. These were VA-46 and VA-72. Before the KENNEDY was to return home from this deployment, these two units would say farewell to the A-7E by flying a combined total of 731 combat missions without a loss.

KENNEDY entered the Red Sea in September 1990 and was joined by the USS AMERICA, CV-66, and the USS SARATOGA, CV-60. These three carriers and their supporting ships formed the Red Sea Battle Force and were commanded by RADM Riley D. Mixson, COMCARGRU TWO embarked in KENNEDY as CTF 155. The air wings from these three carriers conducted practice strikes against Iraqi forces known as Mirror Image operations. In December, KENNEDY paid a port call to Jeddah, Saudi Arabia. She was there on New Year's Day 1991 when Vice President

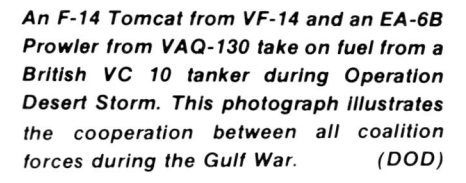

An F-14 Tomcat from VF-14 and an EA-6B Prowler from VAQ-130 take on fuel from a British VC 10 tanker during Operation Desert Storm. This photograph illustrates the cooperation between all coalition forces during the Gulf War. (DOD)

KENNEDY operated the Navy's last two squadrons of A-7E Corsair IIs during Desert Shield and Desert Storm. Here an A-7E from VA-72 is readied for launch on cat one during the war. An AGM-62 Walleye electro-optically guided bomb is attached to the left center wing pylon.
(Official U.S. Navy Photograph)

Quayle visited the ship to show national support for the men deployed in Operation Desert Shield. The following day, KENNEDY again put to sea to resume Mirror Image operations and other training maneuvers as the world waited for Iraq's answer to the January 15, 1991, deadline set by the United Nations for withdrawal of all Iraqi forces from Kuwait.

On January 16, the execute order for Operation Desert Storm was given by President Bush. At 2:57 p.m. local time, RADM Mixson announced to the ship the intention to launch air strikes beginning at 1:20 a.m. on January 17. These opening strikes were launched as scheduled, and all aircraft were safely recovered by 6:00 a.m. Aircrews in the first strike reported heavy but inaccurate anti-aircraft fire.

KENNEDY's crew had welcomed the announcement that strikes would begin with jubilation, not because they were anxious for combat, but because it meant that the seemingly endless period of watching and waiting was finally over. Now something was going to happen, and hopefully it would hasten the day when they could achieve their ultimate goal of getting back home to their families. But the initial jubilation quickly changed to the more serious mood required to accomplish the task at hand. The crews settled into a fast-paced regimen of preparing the strike aircraft, launching them, recovering them, then beginning the process all over again. As each strike launched and returned, everyone held their breath wondering when the air wing would experience its first casualty. Only after 2,895 combat sorties would the crew be able to sigh in collective relief. Although they did not know it the night those first strikes were launched, Carrier Air Wing Three would perform its role in Operation Desert Storm without loss of an aircraft or injury to a crewman.

At the beginning of the Gulf War, KENNEDY, AMERICA, and SARATOGA operated on a six day rotation cycle. Two of the carriers would launch strike aircraft while the third would move to an area in the Red Sea, known as "Gasoline Alley," for two days to replenish munitions, stores, and fuel. This meant that each of the three carriers was on line for four days conducting either a morning (a.m.) or evening (p.m.) flight operations schedule, then off line for two days to replenish. The off line carrier was still tasked with standing anti-air warfare (AAW) and airborne early warning (AEW) alerts, but it did not conduct flight operations against targets in Iraq or Kuwait.

When AMERICA moved from the Red Sea to the Persian Gulf on February 7, KENNEDY and SARATOGA then changed to a different six day cycle. For two days of the six, both carriers were on line, then for the next two days one carrier was off line in "Gasoline Alley." During the last two days of the six day cycle, the other carrier moved off line to replenish. This meant that during the six day cycle there would be two days when both were on line, two days when only KENNEDY was on line, and two days when only SARATOGA was on line.

Aviation ordnancemen fit ADM-141 tactical air-launched decoys to a triple ejector rack on an A-7E of VA-46. These decoys were used to fool enemy radar operators during the war. The decoys appeared to be aircraft on the Iraqi radar scopes, making it impossible for the operators to discern which of their radar returns were actual aircraft.
(Official U.S. Navy Photograph by PH2 William A. Lipski)

This photograph shows GBU-10E laser guided bombs being loaded on Intruders of VA-75. GBU-10s were one of several types of precision guided munitions delivered by the A-6Es against high value targets where pinpoint accuracy was required. The GBU-10E uses the Mk 84, 2000-pound bomb for its warhead.
(Official U.S. Navy Photograph by LCDR Dave Parsons)

When one of the two carriers was off line in gasoline alley, the on line carrier stood all types of alerts, while the off line carrier stood only AAW, AEW, and anti-surface warfare (ASUR) alerts. However, as before, it did not conduct flight operations against targets in Iraq or Kuwait.

Whenever two carriers were on line, two cycles of morning (a.m.) and evening (p.m.) were specified as 0000 to 1500 for the morning carrier and 1200 to 0300 for the evening carrier to accommodate returning strike recovery times. Each carrier usually flew two large strikes with times on target generally being nine hours apart to allow for deck respot and weapons loading. However, combat air patrol (CAP) times were simply midnight to noon and noon to midnight for twelve-hour periods.

The evening carrier was also responsible for pickup of the next day's air tasking order. This had to be picked up in hard copy form because of incompatibility between U.S. Air Force and Navy communications systems. An S-3 Viking from the evening carrier would fly to Riyadh each day, then fly the order back to its carrier. A copy would then be flown to the other carrier(s) by helicopter.

The morning carrier also had to send a Viking to Riyadh each morning by 0700 local time. It carried reconnaissance information on Scud missiles that was collected by F-14 Tomcats using the Tactical Airborne Reconnaissance Pod System (TARPS).

On January 17, KENNEDY launched two major strikes consisting of eighty sorties. This was followed by two more strikes of seventy-two sorties on the 18th of January, and two strikes with seventy sorties the following day. The morning of January 20, KENNEDY launched one strike of forty-six sorties then moved to "Gasoline Alley" to replenish. She returned to combat again on January 22 when she launched one strike of thirty-seven sorties. Carrier Air Wing Three flew two major strikes each day for the next three days, then KENNEDY again took her turn in "Gasoline Alley" to replenish. An A-7E with a failed main landing gear made a successful barricade arrestment while returning from one of the strikes on January 24, but otherwise these missions were flown without incident.

Only seven sorties were flown on January 28, but the next day two strikes of fifty-four sorties were launched against Iraqi ground forces. These missions were flown without any air cover by the ship's fighters, since it had become clear that the Iraqi Air Force had decided not to pose any real threat to the coalition aircraft, particularly above their own troops in Kuwait.

As this cycle of strike operations continued into February, the mood of the crew became somewhat depressed, because they realized that the original February 15 return-from-deployment date would not occur. On that date, there appeared to be a cause for jubilation when Iraq stated its intention to withdraw from Kuwait, but when the conditions attached to this withdrawal became known, the crew realized that they had no cause to celebrate as yet.

With AMERICA now in the Persian Gulf, the pace was even more hectic for both KENNEDY and SARATOGA. Air strikes continued from the ship through the following week and then into the ground assault phase that began on February 24. This time, when news came that Iraq intended to withdraw from Kuwait, the crew was more subdued and had a wait-and-see attitude. But the rout was on, and after only four days of ground fighting, the Iraqis agreed to a cease fire.

As soon as the cease fire was announced, the only thought in the minds of everyone aboard was to return home. Therefore, many were quite frustrated when plans to conduct a first-ever visit by an American warship to Hurghada, Egypt, were announced. This visit began on March 4, and the situation was made worse, because high winds and seas through March 7 caused a cancellation of boating. Finally, KENNEDY left anchorage off Hurghada at midnight on March 10 and prepared to move

AGM-88 HARM anti-radiation missiles are loaded on this Intruder. HARMs were used to suppress and destroy radars that controlled Iraqi surface-to-air missiles and gun systems.
(Official U.S. Navy Photograph by LCDR Dave Parsons)

through the Suez Canal to the Mediterranean Sea.

On March 18, the S-3 Vikings of VS-22 flew off the ship to Sigonella, Italy, then made a trans-Atlantic crossing that saw them arrive back in the United States well ahead of the rest of the ship and CVW-3. Their place was taken on board by AV-8B Harriers from VMA-231 and VMA-542 who flew on for a "lift-of-opportunity" back to Cherry Point MCAS, North Carolina. The Harriers and the rest of Carrier Air Wing Three launched from KENNEDY on March 27 as the ship neared the U.S. coast.

At 2:30 p.m. on March 28, KENNEDY tied up at pier 12 North at the Norfolk Naval Station as she received a welcome from the largest and most enthusiastic crowd to greet an American warship since World War II. A crewman told the author that the shouts of the crowd could be heard on the flight deck as soon as the ship was in sight of the pier, even though the carrier was still over six miles away at the time. KENNEDY's return banner matched the ship's initials with the homecoming theme: "Justice For Kuwait."

The operational record compiled by KENNEDY and Carrier Air Wing Three is indicative of the important role that the Navy's aircraft carriers play in combat. During the forty-two day conflict, CVW-3 flew 114 air strikes consisting of 2,895 combat sorties and a total of 11,263.4 flight hours. Flying to and from their targets in Iraq and Kuwait, the aircraft flew over 2,895,000 miles without loss of aircraft or crew. They expended 3,773,495 pounds of munitions against Iraqi targets, while maintaining a fully mission capable rate of 86.2 percent. The breakdown of sorties by each squadron is as follows:

Squadron	Sorties/Hours
VF-14	371/1324.7
VF-32	372/1354.8
VA-46	369/1611.2
VA-72	362/1548.7
VA-75	
A-6E	417/1882.1
KA-6D	82/271.8
VAW-126	169/720.7
VAQ-130	151/602.2
VS-22	314/1099.7
HS-7	293/847.5

The KENNEDY had eighteen underway replenishments (UNREPS) and seventeen vertical replenishments (VERTREPS) during the Gulf War. VERTREPS are made by helicopters from other ships, while UNREPS are made ship-to-ship. During these replenishments, the carrier took on board 120 tons of fresh fruits and vegetables, 491 tons of dry provisions, 415 tons of frozen provisions, 2,076 pallets and containers of munitions, 4,660,925 gallons of fuel oil and 4,958,314 gallons of JP5 jet fuel.

Upon their return to Norfolk, the crew immediately began a post-deployment standdown, with approximately half of the crew going on leave for one of the two-week leave periods

After delivering over three million pounds of ordnance against Iraqi targets, aircraft of Carrier Air Wing Three rest on the flight deck as the KENNEDY heads home following its seven month deployment in support of Operations Desert Shield and Desert Storm.
(Official U.S. Navy Photograph by PH3 Paul A. Hawthorne)

On October 1, 1991, KENNEDY completed a four month long overhaul at the Norfolk Naval Shipyard. Among the improvements that the ship received during this yard period was the installation of an F/A-18 avionics system in the Aviation Intermediate Maintenance Department. This allowed the F/A-18 Hornet to replace the A-7E in the carrier's air wing. This photograph was taken as tugs maneuvered the carrier out of the shipyard following the overhaul.

(Official U.S. Navy Photograph by PH3 George H. Stuckert)

through the end of April. At the same time, the ship entered a selected restricted availability period and began maintenance, repairs, and an upgrade at the Norfolk Naval Station that lasted until May 28. She then sailed down the Elizabeth River to moor at pier 5 North at the Norfolk Naval Shipyard for more extensive maintenance and upgrades. This yard period had been scheduled for late summer 1990, but Operation Desert Storm had changed all of that.

Among the improvements that were made during this yard period were the reconfiguration of the aircraft maintenance spaces to handle the F/A-18 Hornet, the installation of the NTCS-A command and control system, and the replacement of the non-skid surface on the flight deck and the hangar deck. Extensive repairs were made to the boilers, piping, electrical generators, and air conditioning equipment. Galley and laundry equipment was also replaced.

The yard period lasted until October 1, 1991, when KENNEDY finally left the shipyard and immediately began an at-sea period in the Virginia Capes operating area. She conducted sea trials and recertification for flight deck operations, then commenced fleet carrier qualifications on October 3. After a visit to Port Everglades, Florida, KENNEDY returned home to Norfolk.

On December 3, KENNEDY again put to sea and conducted the first carrier landings and takeoffs by the Navy's new trainer, the T-45 Goshawk II. She returned to Norfolk on December 17 to begin a holiday leave period that was to last until January 6, 1992.

In 1992, KENNEDY again began the rigorous routine followed by all U.S. aircraft carriers. Inspections, qualifying, training, and exercises preceded yet another deployment to the Mediterranean Sea late in the year. As 1992 came to an end and 1993 began, it looked as though the situation in Iraq might require the KENNEDY to become involved in combat again, but things were handled by the USS KITTY HAWK, CV-63, and the U.S. Air Force.

As this is written, KENNEDY remains on deployment, but is scheduled to return soon. After a brief period of rest, the carrier and her crew will once again begin the tough training schedule that keeps both ship and men ready to perform their mission in safeguarding U.S. interests around the world.

Left and above: During December 1991, the T-45A Goshawk II trainer conducted carrier qualifications aboard the KENNEDY. At left, the Goshawk II is being attached to the catapult for launch, while in the photograph above, it catches a wire while making an arrested landing.

(Both are official U.S. Navy Photographs)

SHIP'S STATISTICS

WEIGHTS AND MEASURES

Displacement (full load)	80,073 tons
Displacement (limiting draft)	83,300 tons
Maximum Speed	34+ knots
Design Draft	36.75 feet
Length Overall	1,015.5 feet
Length at Waterline	990 feet
Extreme Breadth at Waterline	129.5 feet
Extreme Breadth at Gallery Walkway	252 feet

HEIGHTS ABOVE WATERLINE

Height of 08 Level	91 feet
Height of 09 Level	98 feet
Height of 010 Level	107 feet
Height of 011 Level	115 feet
Height of Hangar Deck	27 feet
Height of Flight Deck	61 feet
Height of highest Antenna (TACAN)	210 feet

FLIGHT DECK

Total Area	4.56 acres
Axial Deck Length	1,051 feet
Angled Deck Length	760 feet
Arresting Gear Pendant Wires	4
Deck Edge Aircraft Elevators	4
Size of Each Aircraft Elevator	4,000 square feet
Armament Elevators	2
Steam Catapults	4
Aircraft Fueling Stations	26
Aircraft Launching Rate	One every 30 seconds

PROPULSION AND STEERING

Total Shaft Horsepower	280,000
Engine Rooms	4
Boilers	8
Propellers	4
Diameter	21 feet
Blades	5 each
Weight	69,400 pounds each
Rudders	2
Weight	24 tons each
Effective Surface Area	490 square feet

PERSONNEL

Total Enlisted	5,225
Ship's Officers	135
Air Wing's Officers	210

MISCELLANEOUS

Aircraft	90
Compartments	2,023
Anchors	2
Weight of Each Anchor	30 tons
Length of Each Anchor Chain	12 shots, 180 fathoms
Type of Anchor Chain	Die Lock
Life Rafts	333
Electrical Power	
2,500 KW Turbine Driven Generators	6
1,500 KW Emergency Diesel Driven Generators	2
Water Capacity (95%)	
Fresh	369,770 gallons
Feed	178,998 gallons
Fuel Capacity (95%)	
JP-5	1,922,024 gallons
AVGAS*	25,312 gallons
Fuel Oil	2,349,859 gallons

* AVGAS is no longer carried.

CARRIER AIR WING THREE
VF-14 TOPHATTERS

Two F-14As from VF-14 patrol the skies. The Tomcat in the foreground is armed with AIM-7M Sparrow and AIM-54C Phoenix missiles, while the one in the background has an AIM-9M Sidewinder missile on its right glove pylon. The Tophatter's markings are clearly visible on the tail of the aircraft. Since their introduction into service in the early 1970s, Tomcats have been used exclusively in the air-to-air role. However, the airframe's excellent capability to carry and deliver ordnance against surface targets is now being developed. Specially equipped F-14s also use the tactical airborne reconnaissance pod system (TARPS) to perform the tactical reconnaissance mission for the air wing. (USS KENNEDY)

The CAG aircraft from VF-14 is shown here. Its markings are no different than those used on the other aircraft within the squadron.

Number 111 is ready to launch from cat three. Note the angle of the fully raised jet blast deflector behind the aircraft.

VF-32 SWORDSMEN

VF-32 is the other Tomcat squadron in Carrier Air Wing Three. Unlike VF-14, their CAG aircraft is painted in special markings. It is shown here waiting its turn for launch behind the JBD of cat three.

The same aircraft seen above is illustrated again in these two photographs. Note the large red, white, and blue national insignia that is used on this aircraft. At right is a close-up of the tail markings. The entirety of the two vertical tails is painted dark blue, and the markings are yellow. The squadron's name is Swordsmen, and this is lettered vertically down the rudder. The squadron commander's aircraft has similar markings, but its modex is 201.

Except for the CAG and squadron commander's aircraft, all other Tomcats in VF-32 have markings of subdued grays as shown in these two photographs. There is just a hint of pale yellow in the sword on the tail.

VFA-37 BULLS

Two F/A-18C Hornet squadrons have now replaced the two A-7E squadrons that participated in Operation Desert Storm. These are not the same squadrons that have transitioned to a new aircraft. Instead, VA-46 and VA-72 were disestablished after the Gulf War. In the meantime, VFA-37 and VFA-105 were transitioning to the Hornet. These two squadrons had formerly flown the A-7E as part of Carrier Air Wing Six aboard the USS FORRESTAL, CV-59. (See Detail & Scale Volume 36.) This F/A-18C is the CAG aircraft from VFA-36, which is known as the Bulls. The squadron has retained the Schlitz Malt Liquor bull as its emblem on the tail. (USS KENNEDY)

Number 304 taxis across the flight deck to get in position for launch from one of the waist catapults. In the background, two of its squadron mates are already on cats three and four and are almost ready for launch.

Number 305 gets the signal to launch from cat two. (Bell)

This is number 301, which is the squadron commander's aircraft.

VFA-105 GUNSLINGERS

The second Hornet squadron in Carrier Air Wing Three is VFA-105, which is known as the Gunslingers. Four of their aircraft are shown in formation in this photograph.
(USS KENNEDY)

This is the CAG aircraft from VFA-105. The markings are the same as found on the other aircraft in the squadron except that the holster and belt on the tail appear to be a darker gray.

At left is a photograph of the squadron commander's aircraft as it taxis in to position on cat one. At right, number 404 is respotted on the flight deck during a break in flight operations.

VA-75 SUNDAY PUNCHERS

The A-6E squadron in Carrier Air Wing Three is VA-75. The Sunday Punchers provide the air wing with an all-weather attack capability, and they made the first combat launches of the AGM-84E SLAM (Stand-off Land Attack Missile) during Operation Desert Storm. They also delivered a wide variety of other ordnance ranging from Mk 20 Rockeye cluster bombs to the AGM-123A Skipper which is a rocket powered laser guided bomb. Several of the squadron's Intruders can be seen here parked along the edge of the flight deck immediately forward of the superstructure.

Number 514 taxis into position for a launch from cat one.

A-6E, 162192, has a modex of 502 and is shown here tied down on the flight deck. The squadron's tail markings are shown to good effect in this view. The unit insignia is a vertical bomb imposed over a pair of wings, and this marking is visible on the rudder.

Number 512 has been freed from the arresting cable, and is beginning to move out of the landing area to its parking spot. It had been serving as an airborne tanker for other aircraft and was the next to last aircraft down in some rough weather that saw wind speeds in excess of forty knots with gusts as high as seventy knots.

VAQ-130 ZAPPERS

The Zappers of VAQ-130 fly the EA-6B Prowler as part of CVW-3. Their primary mission is to use electronic warfare to protect other aircraft in a strike package from the enemy's radar controlled air defense systems. They can also attack radar sites with anti-radiation missiles. Although the EA-6B first flew in Vietnam, none have ever been lost in combat while performing this dangerous mission. One of VAQ-130's aircraft is shown here armed with an AGM-88 HARM anti-radiation missile. (LT Dave Demauro, VAQ-130)

With three ALQ-99 jamming pods and two external fuel tanks attached to its pylons, EA-6B, 620 waits for its next mission. The marking on the front of the nose is to help the landing signal officer (LSO) identify the aircraft as an EA-6B instead of an A-6E.

EA-6B 624 taxis past a parked F-14A as it moves toward the waist catapults for launch. The aircraft will take off from the carrier, which was operating off the coast of South Carolina when this photograph was taken, then fly all the way across the United States to its home base of Whidbey Island, Washington. It will make two stops along the way.

Number 620 is shown again just seconds before being launched from cat four. Meanwhile, a Tomcat from VF-14 moves in along side to be positioned on cat three.

VS-22 CHECKMATES

The S-3B Viking is flown by the Checkmates of VS-22. The Viking is the dedicated anti-submarine aircraft within the carrier's air wing, and it can also serve as a flying tanker using a buddy refueling store. S-3Bs have been used as surface patrol aircraft, and some attacked surface targets during Operation Desert Storm. Number 706 is still in the gray over white paint scheme, although most markings are in black or gray.
(USS KENNEDY)

Crewmen back an S-3B to the edge of the flight deck prior to running engine checks. Note the protective shields over the engine inlets to prevent a crewman from accidently being sucked into an engine. It is rare to see an aircraft on a carrier with its wings extended except when ready for launch or just after a recovery.

The CAG S-3B from VS-22 is shown here. It is painted overall gray and has all gray and black markings.

Number 704 remains in the gray over white scheme with gray and black markings. Notice how the vertical stabilizer folds to the left. This is particularly helpful when the aircraft is in one of the hangar bays, however, the tail usually is not folded in this manner when the aircraft is on the flight deck.

VAW-126 SEA HAWKS

VAW-126 is the E-2C Hawkeye squadron of CVW-3. The Sea Hawks perform the early warning and airborne control function for the carrier and her air wing. Here, 602 is tied down to the flight deck with its wings folded. Although it is not hooked to the catapult shuttle, the aircraft is spotted at the end of cat three. When air ops begin, it will be in position to be attached to the catapult for immediate launch. Hawkeyes are often the first fixed wing aircraft launched and the last recovered during air operations.

Deck crewmen help guide the wings as they are extended for launch. The engines are already running and the JBD has been raised behind the aircraft. In just a few seconds, the E-2C will be launched as another round of air operations commence.

The small lightning bolts on the side of 603 represent the Hawkeye's participation in Operation Desert Storm.

At left, number 601 catches the number two cable as it recovers between parked aircraft. After coming to a stop, the engines are shut down and the wings are folded. The aircraft is then towed to its parking spot on the flight deck. Because of the high gusty winds and the wet deck conditions that were prevalent when these photographs were taken, a huffer is attached to the tie down at the tail of the aircraft as it is moved across the deck.

23

HS-7 SHAMROCKS

The Shamrocks of HS-7 fly the SH-3H Sea King helicopter as part of CVW-3. The squadron performs the anti-submarine mission as well as search and rescue and plane guard duties.
(USS KENNEDY)

The same helicopter shown above is seen here in its ready position on the angled portion of the flight deck.

Number 610 is parked just aft of the superstructure with its rotor blades and tail section folded for storage.

SHIP'S DETAILS
SUPERSTRUCTURE DETAILS

The original superstructure was far simpler and less cluttered than it is today. This is a port side view showing the island as built. The large radar atop the forward end is the SPS-43, while the SPS-48 is on the lattice mast that is aft of the island.
(National Archives)

This close-up shows the forward and port sides of the superstructure as built. Note that the lower portions of the superstructure were not painted black at first. The camera station is open in this photograph, and the flight deck control station is visible at the forward end of the port side of the island. The 67 is unshaded.
(National Archives)

The starboard side of the superstructure is shown here, and KENNEDY's slanted smokestack is illustrated in good detail. The 67 is large and on the lower portion of the island, and the auxiliary conning station can be seen extending out to starboard from the navigation bridge.
(National Archives)

Today, the port side of the superstructure looks pretty much the way it did originally, except that the lower portion of this side, as well as the forward and aft ends, are painted flat black. Because of the black background, the 67 on this side remains unshaded. BEWARE OF ROTORS PROPS & JET BLAST is painted in yellow to the right of the 67. An SPS-49 radar has replaced the older SPS-43 on top of the forward end of the superstructure.

Considerable changes are apparent in this view of the starboard side of the superstructure when compared to the original configuration that is illustrated on the previous page. Most noteworthy is the addition of the Phalanx gun system and its supporting deck. Another rather large deck has been added just below the flag bridge, and a Mk 78 Sea Sparrow fire control radar has been added atop the auxiliary conning station. ECM antennas extend from the island just above the Phalanx gun mount. Because of the additions to the superstructure, the 67 has been moved to the smokestack. It is outlined with lights and shaded in black.

This front view shows the two bridges to good effect.

This is the aft end of the upper portion of the superstructure showing KENNEDY's slanted smokestack.

The forward end of the port side of the superstructure is shown here. Pri-fly is at the top on the 010 level. Beneath it is the navigation bridge at the 09 level, and below that is the flag bridge at the 08 level. The camera station can be seen with its cover open, and the camera and its operator are visible. The camera station is on the 07 level.

A closer look at the camera station is provided here. In this case the protective cover has been closed.

One of the flag boxes is shown in this view. This is the one on the starboard side of the island.

This photograph was taken at the forward end of the superstructure at the flight deck level, and it looks aft along the starboard side of the island. Note that this face of the superstructure is not painted black. The forward end of the deck for the Phalanx mount is visible, while liters and some small yellow gear can be seen stored on the deck.

The lower portion of the aft end of the island is seen in this view. Some cable rigs are stored here.

BRIDGES

The navigation bridge is at the 09 level on the superstructure. It is shown here fully manned while the ship is at sea.
(National Archives)

At the port end of the navigation bridge is the captain's chair. At left is a view that looks to port from the center of the navigation bridge, and the captain's chair can be seen at the center of the photograph. At right is a close-up of the chair and the area immediately surrounding it.

The engine order telegraph and ship's wheel are shown in this view.

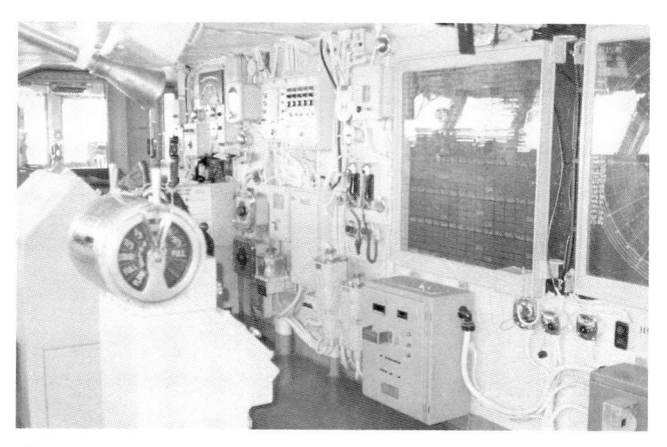

Status boards, telephones, and control panels are located on the wall just behind the ship's wheel and engine order telegraph.

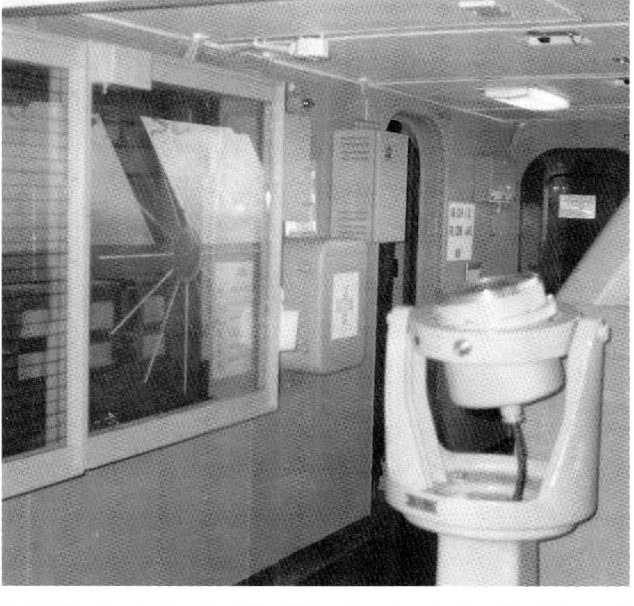

Left: The flag bridge is at the 08 level, and entry is gained through two sets of double doors. These are the doors on the port side. When the admiral and his staff are not embarked, the flag bridge is often used by visitors to watch and photograph air operations.

Above: This picture was taken from the admiral's chair and looks aft along the port side of the flag bridge. In the background are the inside of the same doors which are illustrated in the photograph at left.

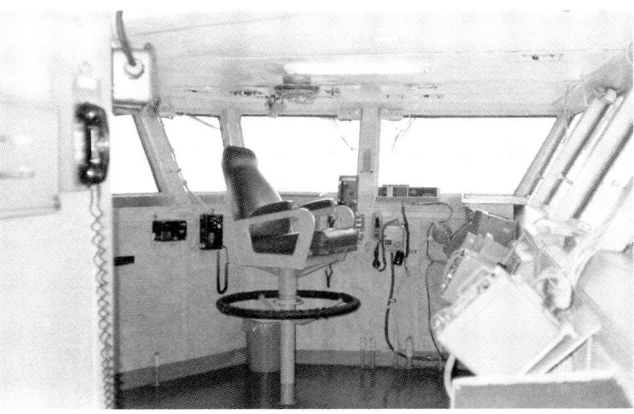

Center left: This is the admiral's chair which is at the port end of the flag bridge. It is directly below the captain's chair that is illustrated on the previous page.

Center right: Taken from the admiral's chair and looking to starboard, this photograph shows the entire width of the flag bridge. At the starboard end is another high swivel chair. The flag bridge is not as large as the navigation bridge and is much simpler.

Left: This is the starboard side of the flag bridge looking aft. The doors for this side of the bridge can be seen in the background.

PRI-FLY

Pri-fly or Primary sits at the 010 level at the forward end of the superstructure. This is the control tower for the ship, and the air boss and mini boss sit next to each other as they control air operations aboard the carrier.

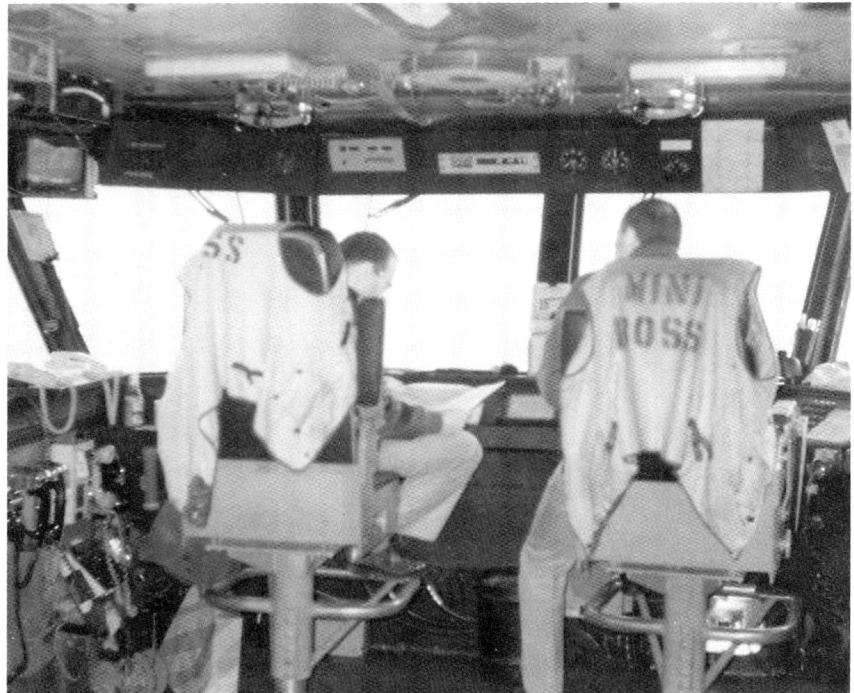

This photograph was taken from the entrance to pri-fly, and shows the air boss and mini boss in their large chairs. This is the part of pri-fly that extends out over the flight deck to port.

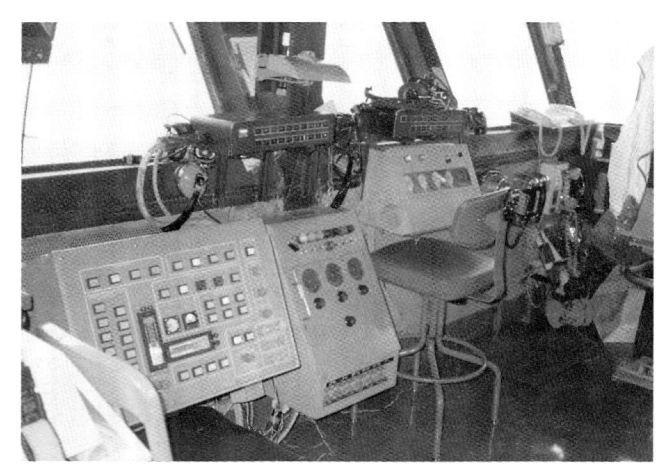

Various control panels are located along the aft end of pri-fly.

This view shows the part of pri-fly that extends forward above the navigation bridge.

30

FLIGHT DECK CONTROL OFFICE

The flight deck control office is at the 04 or flight deck level of the superstructure. It is also known as the Ouija room because of the large board where aircraft symbols are moved around to keep track of where aircraft are located on the flight deck and the hangar deck. This is one of the entrances to the flight deck control office. (National Archives)

A wedged shaped area of the flight deck control office extends out to port from the superstructure. Large square windows with very thick glass provide personnel inside the office with a view of the flight deck.

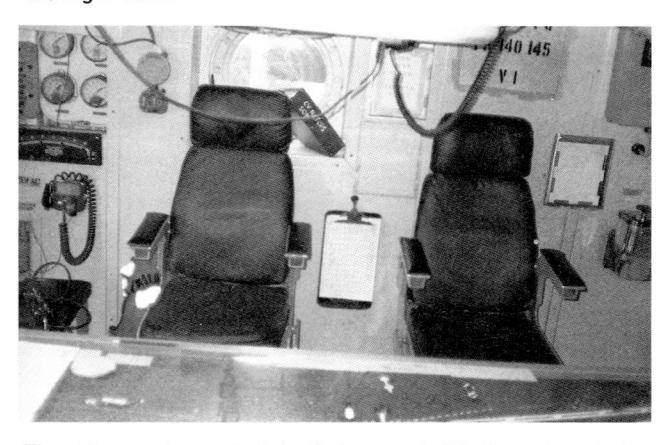

The officers who control the Ouija board sit in these two chairs. Behind them is a porthole that looks forward on to the flight deck.

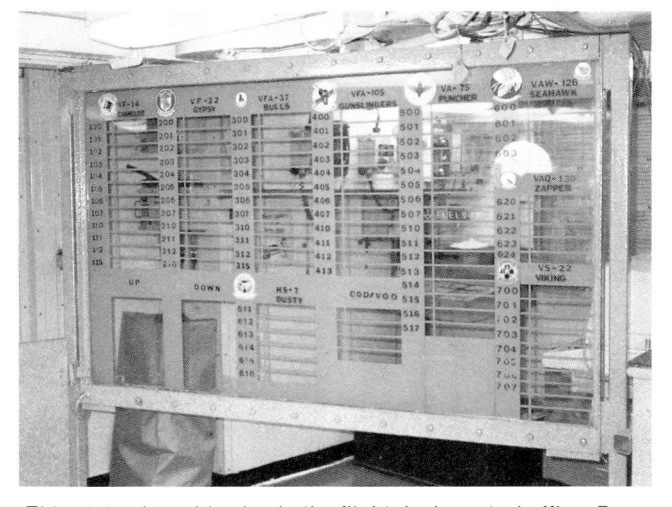

Here, the flight deck control office is shown fully manned during air operations. The two levels of the Ouija board can be seen, and personnel are moving aircraft symbols on the board to represent the positions of the aircraft on the two decks. The modex of each aircraft is written on its corresponding symbol.
(Official U.S. Navy Photograph by PH2 Leo Latasiewicz)

This status board is also in the flight deck control office. Every squadron and every aircraft is represented by its modex on this board. A recorder stands behind the board and keeps track of each of the aircraft. Using a grease pencil, he writes the status backward on the plexiglass, thus making it readable for the personnel in front of the board.

BOW DETAILS

Bow details are visible in this view which was taken while the ship was in port. Both of the KENNEDY's two anchors can be seen as can the single remaining catapult overrun on the bow. The five portholes for the secondary conning station are located on the facing just below the flight deck level.

The bulbous shape of the bow dome can be seen in this photograph that was taken while the ship was in drydock. The view looks down from in front of the ship's stem. (USS KENNEDY)

These two photographs show left and right side views of the bow below the waterline. Both the hull red anti-fouling bottom paint and the black boot topping had just been freshly painted when these photos were taken. The keel blocks are visible in both views, and the depth markings can be seen in the photo at right. (Both USS KENNEDY)

Coverage of the ship's details continues on page 41.

COLOR GALLERY

In her early days, the USS JOHN F. KENNEDY was almost devoid of any color. Except for a darker gray landing area, even the flight deck was approximately the same color as the vertical surfaces. The 67 at the forward end of the flight deck is gray and is difficult to see. It was painted white shortly after these photos were taken. These two views show KENNEDY's details and colors as built.
(Both National Archives)

Above and right: The photograph above was shot from a different angle than the two views shown on the previous page, however, it was taken on the same day and illustrates the same colors and markings. By contrast, the photograph at right was taken a few months later, and shows the flight deck markings that were added when the carrier was ready to start operating aircraft. A prominent solid white 67 is now visible at the forward end of the flight deck, and the landing area has been bordered by large white markings. It has a centerline of alternating yellow and white segments. The four elevators appear to be a little darker than the rest of the deck, and they are outlined with stripes of alternating red and yellow colors. During the ship's early days, the covers for the two armament elevators were painted solid white. Note that the defensive armament of three Mk 25 BPDMS launchers has yet to be added. (Both National Archives)

The USS JOHN F. KENNEDY had become a commissioned ship in the U.S. Navy by the time this photograph was taken, and elements of her first air wing are visible on her flight deck. These aircraft include Skywarriors, Skyhawks, Vigilantes, and Phantoms. Also note that the three BPDMS launchers are now in place. The markings on the island and flight deck remain the same, as shown in the top right photograph. (National Archives)

This starboard view was taken as the KENNEDY departed Norfolk for Operations Desert Shield and Desert Storm. It shows the ship in its present configuration. (Official U.S. Navy Photograph)

Present port side colors and details of KENNEDY are revealed in this photograph that was taken on April 15, 1992. (Bell)

Taken from a much higher angle than the photograph directly above, this view shows the present flight deck markings to good effect. With only four aircraft on the flight deck, almost all of the markings are visible. The wavy lines on the deck are made by crewmen washing down the deck with hoses. When this photo was taken the ship was at anchor, and the anchor chain can be seen extending from the bow into the water.
(Bell)

FIREPOWER

As is the case with any aircraft carrier, the main component of the ship's firepower, both offensive and defensive, is found in the air wing. Exemplifying Carrier Air Wing Three's striking power, this large bomb symbol is painted on both sides of KENNEDY's superstructure. It records that CVW-3 flew 114 air strikes and expended 3,773,495 pounds of ordnance against Iraqi targets during Operation Desert Storm.

For close-in defense against anti-ship missiles and aircraft, three Phalanx gun systems have been added to the ship's armament. One of the gun mounts is shown here during a practice exercise.
(Official U.S. Navy Photograph)

Marines practice firing one of several .50 calibre machine guns that are located around the ship. These old but reliable guns have reappeared as part of the ship's armament to be used against terrorists in small craft or on the shore when the ship is in port. This particular mount is located on the fantail.
(Official U.S. Navy Photograph)

Mk 29 Sea Sparrow launchers have replaced the older and larger Mk 25 launchers on the KENNEDY. In the photograph at left, crewmen load a missile into one of the three launchers. At right a practice missile is fired from the launcher on the starboard quarter.
(Left Official U.S. Navy Photograph, right USS KENNEDY)

DETAILS IN COLOR

Taken while the ship was in drydock, the photographs on this page provide excellent detailed views of the two rudders and four propellers. Note that the two propellers on the starboard side rotate clockwise, while the two on the port side rotate counter-clockwise to propel the ship forward. Depth markings on the left side of the hull and at the centerline of the stern are visible in this view. (USS KENNEDY)

The inner shaft and propeller on the port side are shown here as is the port rudder. Note that the propeller is polished magnesium bronze, while the shaft is gray. The braces for the shaft are hull red. (USS KENNEDY)

More details of the propellers and rudders are shown in these two views. The men in the photograph at right provide a size comparison for the huge five-bladed propellers and the rudders. Each propeller or screw is twenty-one feet in diameter and weighs 69,400 pounds. Each rudder weighs approximately twenty-four tons, and they have an effective area of 490 square feet. (Both USS KENNEDY)

AIR OPS---PAST

Two A-7Bs from VA-46 prepare for launch from cats one and two. The Clansmen of VA-46 would remain part of the KENNEDY's air wing until they were disestablished after Operation Desert Storm.
(National Archives)

A deck crewman checks the bridle as an F-4N Phantom is readied for launch. Note the holdback cable behind the aircraft and the early short jet blast deflector.
(National Archives)

A Skywarrior, more commonly known as the "whale," is checked over on the flight deck. In the background, crewmen do a FOD walkdown, before the start of flight operations. They are looking for any debris on the flight deck that might be sucked into the jet engines and cause damage.
(National Archives)

AIR OPS---PRESENT

With a burst of steam and an ear piercing roar, the CAG F-14A from VF-14 is launched on cat three.

The CAG F/A-18C from VFA-37 taxis across the flight deck toward the waist catapults.

An F/A-18C from VFA-105 moves through the steam on to cat one. Note the deck crewman standing in the steam to direct the aircraft on to the catapult. All three photographs on this page were taken on April 14, 1992, as the entire air wing launched from the carrier, and the aircraft headed for their various home stations.

An E-2C Hawkeye from VAW-126 is about to launch from cat three as one of HS-7's Sea Kings hovers close by as a plane guard. Plane guard helicopters usually orbit on the starboard side of the ship.

Armed with an AGM-88 HARM anti-radiation missile, an A-6E Intruder from VA-75 moves forward to cat one under the watchful eye of deck crewmen.

An EA-6B Prowler from VAQ-130 is only seconds away from launch on cat three.

The pilot of an S-3B Viking of VS-22 checks out his controls before being hooked up to cat one.

Although not part of the carrier's air wing, a frequent and welcome visitor is a C-2A Greyhound from VRC-40. These COD aircraft shuttle mail, passengers, and cargo between the ship and the shore. Here a C-2A taxis to a parking spot on the number two elevator after landing aboard CV-67.

40

ANCHORS & FOS'CLE

KENNEDY has two anchors, one of which is located on the starboard side of the bow in the conventional manner. The other is on a stem hawsepipe directly on the front of the bow. This arrangement was necessary because of the sonar dome below the waterline, but the sonar was deleted. Both anchors, each weighing thirty tons, are shown in this general view.

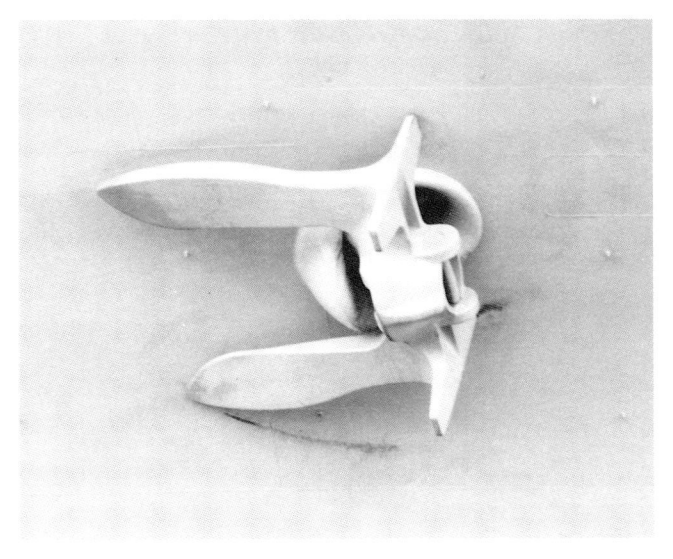

At left is a close-up view of the starboard anchor, while details of the stem anchor and its hawsepipe are visible in the photograph at right.

This photo was taken at the forward end of the fos'cle and looks aft. The forward anchor chain can be seen to the right, and the chain for the starboard anchor exits the fos'cle through the covered opening to the left.

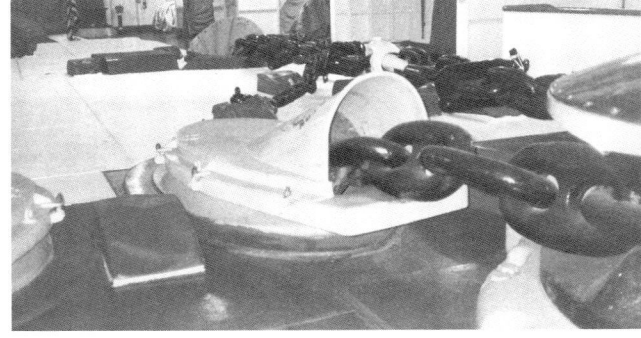

More details of the chain for the starboard anchor are shown here. The chain goes out to the anchor through the opening in the background, while it is stored in a space directly below the fos'cle. It exits the fos'cle and goes down to the storage area through the covered opening in the foreground. Each chain is long enough to allow use of the anchors in up to 180 fathoms of water.

FLY AROUND

On this page and the next, details of the KENNEDY are studied in a fly around made by the author in a helicopter. The fly around begins with the port bow and moves counter-clockwise around to the starboard bow. In this view the forward Phalanx mount and its supporting sponson are visible ahead of the angled area of the flight deck. Note the catapult overrun for cat three at the extreme right in the photograph.

About half way back under the port side overhang is a boat deck with a small whaleboat stored at its forward end. Directly above it is the fresnel lens system at the flight deck level. The barrel-shaped items mounted in pairs along the catwalks are self-inflating life rafts. There are a total of 333 of these rafts on the ship.

Further aft is another cutout in the structure that supports the flight deck overhang on the port side. It has a small deck on which numerous fifty-five gallon drums are stored. A portion of the number four elevator can be seen to the right in this photograph. The white object in the catwalk at the extreme left of the photograph is one of two SMQ-10 or "SMACK-10" weather satellite tracking antennas. The other SMQ-10 is on the starboard side of the ship.

Details of the port quarter are visible here. A Phalanx gun mount can be seen at the aft end of the ship, while just forward of it is a larger sponson supporting a Mk 29 Sea Sparrow launcher and its two associated radars. Just forward of that sponson is the LSO platform. The number four elevator is at the far left in this photograph.

This is the starboard quarter. Visible are the ship's crane and the sponsons that support another Sea Sparrow launcher and its two radars. The radars are in a stepped arrangement on this side. Part of the number three elevator can be seen at right.

This is the starboard side amidships. The number three elevator is to the left, and the number two elevator is to the right. Between them is the supporting structure for the starboard overhang and superstructure. A small cutout for a whaleboat can be seen at the aft end of the supporting structure. The opening just below the lattice radar mast that appears as a large backward L is where the replenishment lines are stored. The Phalanx mount on the starboard side of the island is visible in this view, and the square white objects below it are lockers for pyrotechnic devices.

Elevators number two (left) and number one (right) can be seen in this photograph. Between them at the hangar deck level is the quarterdeck. Above it in the catwalk is the second SMQ-10 weather satellite tracking antenna.

This is the starboard bow. The swallow's nest for the forward Sea Sparrow launcher is visible, but its two associated radars are located on the superstructure. More details of the starboard side can be seen in the photographs on the following page.

43

STARBOARD SIDE DETAILS

Above: Better details of the quarterdeck can be seen in this photograph that was taken while the ship was in port. It is located between elevators one and two at the hangar deck level, and it is where officers and VIPs board and exit the ship.

Right: Replenishment lines can be seen hanging from their overhead racks in this photograph that was taken from the number three elevator while the ship was at sea.
(Official U.S. Navy Photograph by PH3 Milton Savage)

The opening for the replenishment lines shown in the top right photograph is illustrated here in better detail. Also visible is the cutout for the starboard whaleboat.

This small deck is sponsored out from the forward end of the structure that supports the starboard overhang amidships. It is used extensively during underway replenishments at sea called UNREPS.

This close-up provides a good look at the details of the starboard quarter.

Details of the ship's crane are shown here. The crane is often used while the ship is in port to move heavy items on to or off of the number three elevator. The Sea Sparrow launcher and one of its radars can be seen in the upper left hand corner of the photograph.

WEAPONS SYSTEMS

BASIC POINT DEFENSE MISSILE SYSTEM

The first defensive armament carried by the KENNEDY consisted of three Mk 25 Basic Point Defense Missile System (BPDMS) launchers. This system was the forerunner to the NATO Sea Sparrow Missile System (NSSMS) used today. The larger Mk 25 box launcher was required, because the missiles did not have the folding wings of the present missiles. The early system also had a less sophisticated guidance system and did not require the Mk 78 radars to guide the missiles. This photograph shows a BPDMS (pronounced bee-pee-dee-muss) missile being fired from the forward launcher during a practice exercise. (National Archives)

Center above: Another missile is shown being fired from the Mk 25 launcher on the starboard quarter. The large box launcher and its supporting sponson are clearly visible in this view. It was supported by the same structure that also acted as a rest for the ship's crane. (National Archives)

Left: This close-up view of a missile firing from the forward launcher shows how the front cover of the launcher broke away as the missile was fired. (USS KENNEDY)

MARK 29 NATO SEA SPARROW MISSILE SYSTEM

The original BPDMS was replaced with the much improved NATO Sea Sparrow Missile System with its smaller Mk 29 launchers and associated Mk 78 radar systems. Each Mk 29 has two radars, so additions were made to the two sponsons on the quarters to allow the radars to be positioned in close proximity to the new Mk 29s. This is the launcher and its two radars on the port quarter.

This close-up reveals more details of the launcher on the port quarter. Each side of the launcher contains four missiles for a total of eight.

The two continuous wave Mk 78 radars for the launcher on the port quarter are shown here on their two small platforms. They are pointed skyward while undergoing checks. The convex or right side of each radar is the transmitter, while the concave or left side is the receiver. These radars illuminate the targets with radar beams, and the missiles home in on the energy from these beams that is reflected by the targets.

This is the launcher on the starboard quarter. Its two associated radars are configured in a stepped arrangement on a separate sponson that is just below and aft of the platform for the launcher.

This photograph was taken from the flight deck, and shows the same launcher from above.

These two views show the Mk 29 on the starboard bow. Unlike the two launchers on the quarters, the radars associated with this launcher are not located near it, but are on the superstructure instead. One is atop the auxiliary conning station, and the other is just above and behind it on its own small sponson. These two radars can be seen in the photographs of the superstructure on pages 27 and 43.

MARK 15 PHALANX CLOSE-IN WEAPON SYSTEM

There are three Mk 15 Phalanx Close-In Weapon Systems (CIWS) positioned around the ship to provide defense against anti-ship missiles and low flying aircraft. This 20 mm gun system is based on the six-barrel Vulcan cannon, and has proven to be very effective even in the presence of electronic countermeasures. This is the Phalanx mount on the port bow. Also note the RBOC chaff launcher on the near side of the supporting sponson.

Above and right: These two views show the Phalanx mount on the starboard side of the superstructure. Each Phalanx mount is completely self-contained, and includes the gun, ammunition storage drum, and radar system. The radar is in the white dome at the top of the mount.

The Phalanx mount on the port quarter is illustrated in these two photographs. At left is a view from above and looking down at the mount from the Sea Sparrow launcher. At right is a photograph of the same mount being fired during a practice exercise.

(Left author, right USS KENNEDY)

.50 CALIBER MACHINE GUNS

Positions for .50 caliber machine guns are located around the ship. These guns are intended for use against terrorist attacks in small craft or from the shore while the ship is in port. At left is a mount that is being fired in practice by Marines. When not needed, the machine guns are stowed away, and only their shields and mounts remain in place. At right is a photo of one of the mounts that is located in the catwalk along the flight deck. (Left USS KENNEDY, right author)

MARK 36 RAPID BLOOM OFFBOARD CHAFF SYSTEM

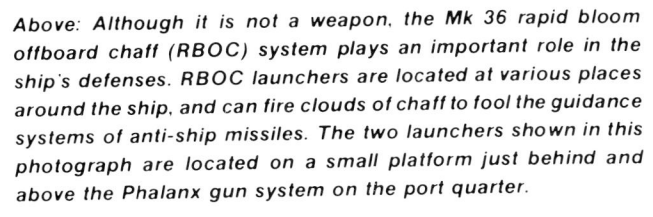

Above: Although it is not a weapon, the Mk 36 rapid bloom offboard chaff (RBOC) system plays an important role in the ship's defenses. RBOC launchers are located at various places around the ship, and can fire clouds of chaff to fool the guidance systems of anti-ship missiles. The two launchers shown in this photograph are located on a small platform just behind and above the Phalanx gun system on the port quarter.

Above right: These RBOC launchers are on the starboard quarter just aft of the Sea Sparrow launcher.

Right: More RBOC launchers are located on the starboard side of the superstructure.

49

MAST & PRIMARY RADARS

Above: The AN/SPS-49 radar is mounted on top of the forward end of the superstructure and is used for long range air search.

Right: This view of the mast was taken from the port side and shows over a dozen antennas of all types. The TACAN is mounted at the very top of the mast over two-hundred feet above the waterline, and the circular radar just above and in front of the flag is the AN/WSC-3 or "Whiskey-3" antenna that is used for VHF communications. The large gray antenna on the platform that extends aft from the mast is the AN/SPN-43 close-in low level air search radar, and the bar-like antenna just a little lower on the platform that extends forward from the mast is for the Mk 48 target acquisition system (TAS).

Taken from the starboard side of the mast, these two photographs show additional details of the AN/SPN-43 (left) and the Mk 48 antenna (right). Note the waveguides and the dozens of cables that run up this side of the mast to the various antennas.

These two views show the lattice radar mast abaft the island with its AN/SPS-48 radar at its mast head and the elevation dome for the SPN-41 automatic landing control radar near its base.

Details of the AN/SPS-48 radar antenna are shown in these two close-up photographs.

The elevation dome for the SPN-41 automatic landing control radar is mounted about fifteen feet up on the lattice mast. The azimuth dome is on the fantail and is illustrated on page 65.

The two identical antennas located one above the other are AN/SPN-42 radars that are associated with the automatic carrier landing system. The smaller dish antenna to the left is the AS/SPN-44 that measures the speed of incoming aircraft as they make their approach to land.

51

FLIGHT DECK DETAILS

CATWALKS

This is the catwalk that runs along the forward edge of the flight deck on the starboard side. What appears to be two round eyes near the center of the photograph are infrared lights, and between them is a camera that photographs aircraft as they are launched from catapult number one. Just beyond the camera is the bomb chute that is illustrated in the photograph at right.

At various places around the flight deck are these chutes where ordnance can be pushed overboard in the event of a fire. These chutes were added when difficulty was experienced in throwing ordnance overboard during fires aboard FORRESTAL and ENTERPRISE.

Two saluting guns are located in the catwalk on the starboard side where the flight deck widens to its full width. The forward Sea Sparrow launcher can be seen in the background.

After the KENNEDY's collision with the BELKNAP, a pole mast was added to all U.S. carriers. Known as the KENNEDY or BELKNAP pole, it too is located on the catwalk where the flight deck widens on the starboard side, and it is directly forward of the superstructure. Navigation lights are mounted on this pole mast to aid other ships in determining the carrier's heading at night. This is done by comparing the relative position of the lights on this pole to the navigation light at the masthead of the main mast. A relative wind speed and direction indicator is located at the top of the pole mast.

At various places in the catwalks around the flight deck are refueling stations like this one. In all, KENNEDY has twenty-six refueling stations. This station is located in the catwalk at the extreme aft end of the flight deck on the port side.

This is the LSO platform as seen from behind and looking forward.

Next to the hook-up position for cat four is a small platform that has been added to the edge of the flight deck. It provides a place for deck crewmen to stand during launches without them having to constantly climb down into and back out of the catwalks.

Another view of the LSO platform shows the wind over the deck (WOD) shield with its four windows. Covered netting surrounds the LSO platform. In the event of an emergency, the LSOs can jump into this covered netting and slide down below the platform out of harm's way.

At a point further forward on the port side of the flight deck is the fresnel lens system. At left is a look at the light arrangement that signals the pilot if he is on the proper approach for landing. At right is a view from a position forward of the lens looking back at the shield that protects it.

53

In the foreground is the catapult overrun for cat three, while in the background is the catwalk that runs along the forward edge of the flight deck on the port side.

This view looks forward along the catwalk shown in the photograph at left. In the foreground is a reel with a water hose that is used for washing down the deck or for fighting fires. In the background are more reels with hoses for refueling aircraft.

Not all refueling points are in the catwalks. This one is located under the flight deck just in front of the superstructure. Hoses have been pulled out of the refueling station and placed on the deck. A water hose and its reel can be seen on the forward face of the superstructure in the background.

This is a close-up view of the camera that records launches from cat two. It has the two infrared lights with the camera between them as discussed on page 52.

At various places around the flight deck are small hatches that cover high pressure air supplies and electrical connections. At left is one of these locations with the hatch closed, while at right a crewman removes a large compressed air hose that is used for starting jet engines. Also inside the compartment are electrical cables that can provide electrical power to aircraft.

ARMAMENT ELEVATORS

There are two armament elevators that move ordnance and other items between the flight deck and the magazines below. One is located forward between cats one and two and can be seen in this photograph. The cover for the elevator is outlined in a solid white line which in turn is outlined with a wider line of alternating red and yellow segments.

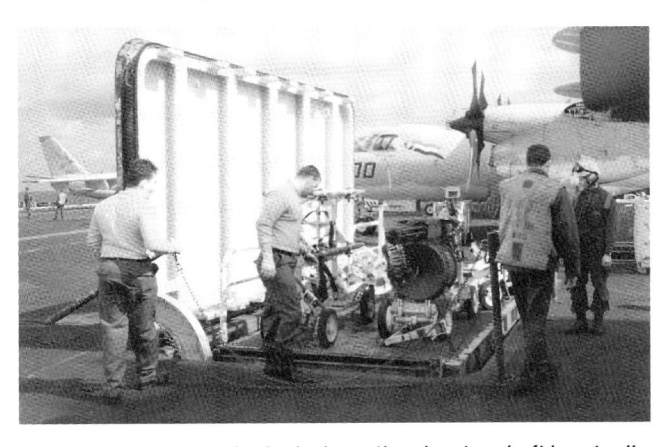

The portion of the flight deck above the elevator shaft is actually a cover that hinges open, as illustrated in this view. Some small yellow gear is positioned on the elevator, and one of the pieces of equipment is loaded with the gun system from an F/A-18C Hornet.

This view looks down at the elevator as it descends to the magazine. The gun system for the F/A-18C is clearly visible.

The second armament elevator is located just aft of the superstructure. When an armament elevator is to be used, poles with chains are positioned around it as shown here to prevent personnel from falling into it. There are no retractable cable railings around these elevators as there are around the four aircraft elevators.

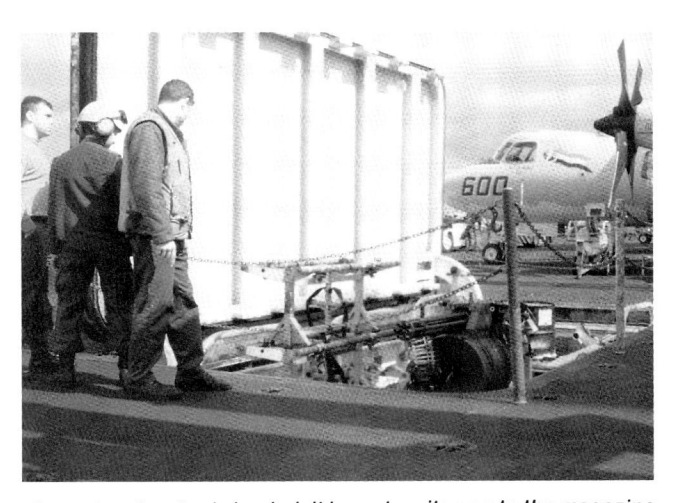

Once the elevator is loaded, it is sent on its way to the magazine below.

Once the elevator has descended far enough, the cover at the flight deck level closes over the opening. A portion of the cable system that raises and lowers the elevator can be seen in this view. The cover is strong enough to allow any aircraft or piece of equipment to be rolled over it during air operations or other flight deck activities.

55

CATAPULTS

Like all presently active aircraft carriers in the U.S. Navy, the KENNEDY has four steam catapults numbered from one to four from starboard to port. Therefore, the two bow catapults are one and two. Here an A-6E Intruder prepares to depart on cat one, while an F/A-18C Hornet is in position on cat two. Both JBDs are raised to their full up position to protect personnel and other aircraft behind the catapults as the aircraft run their engines up to take-off power.

On older aircraft a rather complex system of bridles and holdback cables was used to attach them to the catapult. Here a deck crewman checks the bridle on a Skywarrior prior to launch. The smaller cables extending from the bridle down to the deck are attached to two other cables that run along the sides of the catapult track. This system pulled the bridle free of the aircraft at the end of the catapult, and it also prevented the bridle from going overboard. The holdback cable can be seen at the far right in the photograph. (National Archives)

Today a far simpler and more efficient nose wheel tow system is used. An arm on the nose wheel is attached to the catapult shuttle as shown in this view. The holdback bar (not visible in this photograph) is hooked behind the nose wheel to the catapult. This eliminates the need for the heavy bridles that must be carried back to the hookup end of the catapult by deck personnel after each launch. (National Archives)

The catapults are fired from positions in the catwalks. The crewman who fires the catapult holds his hands in the air until all other crewmen are clear of the aircraft and he receives the signal from the catapult officer to launch the aircraft.

(National Archives)

56

Cat one is the only catapult remaining on the KENNEDY that can use the old bridle launch system. Cleats for the holdback cables are located at the hookup end of the catapult as shown here.

At the other end of cat one is the bridle arrestor and catapult overrun, as explained on the previous page.

The proper amount of steam pressure for cats one and two is ordered from this location in the flight deck between the two catapults. The amount of pressure required depends on the gross weight of the aircraft.

There are no holdback cleats at the hookup end of cat two, so only aircraft with the nose wheel tow system can be launched from this catapult. All aircraft in the Navy's carrier air wings now use this system, so the cleats and the overrun at the other end have been removed.

This view looks aft from the forward end of cat two. Unlike cat one, cat two ends short of the forward end of the flight deck as shown here.

57

The two waist catapults are numbered three and four. Here a Tomcat is shown hooked up to cat three, and the jet blast deflector (JBD) has been raised in position to deflect the jet blast upwards. Contrary to what some people may think, the JBD is not raised to a ninety degree angle to the flight deck. This would put too much pressure on it from the jet engines and would deflect the blast back toward the aircraft and its engine nozzles.

Cat four runs right along the port side of the flight deck. There is just enough room for the left main landing gear of the aircraft to fit on the deck when being launched from this catapult.

This is a rear view of the JBD behind cat three.

Steam pressure for cats three and four is ordered from this position in the flight deck. It is located between the two catapults, and is the same as the one illustrated on the previous page for cats one and two. The two waist catapults are fired from positions in the port side catwalk.

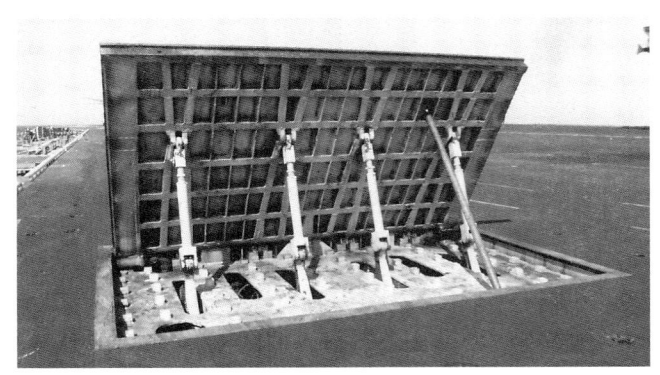

Because cat four is so close to the edge of the flight deck, a much smaller JBD is used behind it. Unlike the other JBDs which have six sections, this JBD is a single piece. It is also much shorter than the other deflectors. At left is a front view of the JBD behind cat four, and at right is a rear view.

58

LANDING AREA

ARRESTING CABLES

The tail hook of an EA-6B Prowler is only inches above the flight deck as the aircraft makes a recovery aboard the KENNEDY. The number two wire is just below the aircraft on the flight deck.
(Official U.S. Navy Photograph)

An A-7E comes to a halt after catching the wire. The LSOs record the landing, including which cable was caught by the aircraft's tail hook. Pilots are constantly critiqued and graded on their recoveries aboard ship.
(Official U.S. Navy Photograph)

The four arresting cables are controlled from this position in the starboard catwalk. After a cable is freed from the aircraft, it is retracted and made ready for the next recovery.

There are four arresting gear engine rooms--one for each cable. They are located on the 03 level directly below the flight deck. The hydraulic engines are set according to the weight of the recovering aircraft.

59

The cross deck pendant is the part of the cable that stretches across the flight deck. In the center it is supported several inches off of the deck by flat leaf springs.

When an aircraft catches the cable, the terminals will hit the deck quite hard as the plane comes to a stop. To help protect the deck, terminal impact pads, which are made of hard rubber, are placed by each fair lead sheave at about a forty-five degree angle as shown here. This not only protects the deck but the terminals as well.

The cross deck pendant is attached to a purchase cable at each end. The purchase cable is the part that extends down to the arresting gear engine room below. The purchase cables are joined to the cross deck pendant by terminals. These are large metal links, one of which can be seen in this photograph.

The point where the cable goes into the flight deck is called a fair lead sheave, and these are retractable as shown here. During recovery operations, the fair lead sheaves would be extended up from the flight deck to help hold the cable several inches above the deck.

After recording a specified number of recoveries, the purchase cables are removed on a reel like this one. They are either replaced or inspected and load tested before being reused.

CRASH BARRIER

Sometimes an aircraft is unable to make a normal arrested recovery and must "take the barricade" instead. There are three crash barricades or barriers that are kept in a space just below the flight deck about even with the number four arresting cable. The bottom barricade is used only for practice and training by flight deck personnel. The barricade in the middle is used for the emergency recovery of jet aircraft, while the one on top is used for propeller driven aircraft like the E-2C or C-2A.

A hatch leads down to the room where the barricades are stored. In the event of an emergency, the proper barricade can be pulled up out of the storage area and rigged in a matter of minutes.

In the photograph at left, crewmen are shown rigging the barricade, while at right is a photo of the barricade fully rigged and erected. (Both are Official U.S. Navy Photographs by PH1 Michael D. P. Flynn)

While the two photographs above show the barricade being rigged for practice, in this case it was no drill. An A-7E is brought to a stop by the barricade with relatively little damage and no injury to its pilot or flight deck personnel. The aircraft was repaired to fly another day. (USS KENNEDY)

ELEVATORS

As is the case with all aircraft carriers in the U.S. Navy, KENNEDY has four large aircraft elevators. Each measures over 4,000 square feet in area. The elevator arrangement is the same as it is on all U.S. carriers except for the four ships of the FORRESTAL class. There are three elevators on the starboard side numbered one, two, and three from fore to aft. Two are forward of the superstructure and one is aft. The only elevator on the port side is elevator number four. Elevators one and two can be seen in this view. A line of alternating red and yellow segments marks off the elevator, while a second outer line of red and yellow marks the location of the retractable railing around the elevator. This railing is simply a series of poles with a cable running along their tops.

The number two elevator is shown from below in the raised position. The oval opening to the hangar bay is clearly visible, as are some of the beams that provide strength underneath the elevator.

An S-3B Viking is backed out of the forward hangar bay on to elevator number one. Note the cables that raise and lower the elevator next to the aircraft's right wing fold. There are four sets of these cables for each elevator. Also note the red and yellow markings on the deck and elevator. The railing of retractable poles and a cable at the flight deck level can be seen at the top of the photograph.

This is elevator number one as seen while the ship was in port. The elevator is in the lowered position, and again the cables that raise and lower it are visible.

This close-up shows the protective sliding doors almost closed over one of the openings to the hangar bays. Quite often the doors are left open just a little, as they are here, in order to provide some cross ventilation of the hangar deck.

Elevator number three is located aft of the superstructure. It is shown here in the lowered position. The ship's crane is being used to move heavy items from the pier on to the elevator.

This view looks down and aft at the lowered number three elevator from the flight deck.

This is the lowered number three elevator as seen from behind. A gangway has been placed on the elevator to allow crewmen to board or leave the carrier.

It is difficult to get photographs showing the number four elevator from the side, because carriers berth with their starboard side to the pier. Therefore, you need a boat or an aircraft to get a good picture of the port elevator. This photograph was taken from a helicopter.

HANGAR BAYS

The hangar deck on the KENNEDY begins just forward of the opening for the number one elevator and extends aft almost to the stern. The jet engine maintenance shop is located between the aft end of the hangar deck and the fantail. The hangar deck is divided into two bays which can be separated by large blast doors. Approximately twenty-five aircraft can be placed in the two bays at any one time. Maintenance is performed on the hangar deck that could not be done on the flight deck while aircraft were exposed to the elements. This photograph was taken early in the KENNEDY's service life and shows the hangar deck crowded with aircraft. In the photograph are several Phantoms, a Vigilante, a Skywarrior, and a Tracer. Except for two whaleboats, all of the ship's boats and the captain's launch are stored on the hangar deck in addition to the aircraft. (National Archives)

With all of the aircraft removed, more details of the hangar deck can be seen in this photograph. The hangar deck is 688 feet long and 106 feet wide. Its overhead clearance is twenty-five feet. A lot of yellow gear and other equipment can be seen in the photo. This view looks aft from the forward end of the hangar deck. (National Archives)

An A-6E Intruder gets a complete going over by maintenance personnel. Note that the hangar deck has the same tie downs (known as pad eyes) as the flight deck and also has the same dark gray non-skid surface. (National Archives)

This Tomcat is spotted at the aft end of bay two next to the opening for the number three elevator. (National Archives)

FANTAIL & STERN

A good overall look at the stern as it appears today is shown in this view.

The ship's name is lettered on the aft end of the jet engine test area which projects aft from the fantail.

This photograph shows the original or "as built" configuration of KENNEDY's stern. Note the stairs (ladder in Navy terminology) that fold down out of the sponson for the jet engine test bed. This provides easy access to the captain's launch or the other ship's boats when the carrier is anchored off shore.

(National Archives)

The vertical bar is painted yellow and is part of the series of landing lights that line up with the centerline on the flight deck above. The break in the middle is for the azimuth dome of the SPN-41 automatic carrier landing system.

BELOW DECKS

The KENNEDY's Combat Direction Center (CDC) is shown in this photograph. It is from here that all of the ship's systems are monitored and controlled during combat.
(National Archives)

The carrier's air traffic control center keeps track of all of the aircraft in the air.

There are a lot of radar scopes in the air operations department as seen in these two photographs, but not everything is sophisticated and automated. A small television camera can be seen hanging down from the ceiling and is aimed at a small representation of the ship's landing pattern. This is clearly visible between the two radar scopes to the left in the photograph at right. A crewman manually positions representations of aircraft on the diagram of the landing pattern as the actual aircraft fly the same pattern around the ship. The representations of the aircraft have the modex numbers written on them to identify which aircraft is which. The overhead television camera continually transmits an image of this manually operated apparatus to various places in the ship so those who need to know can keep track of the location of each aircraft in the pattern.

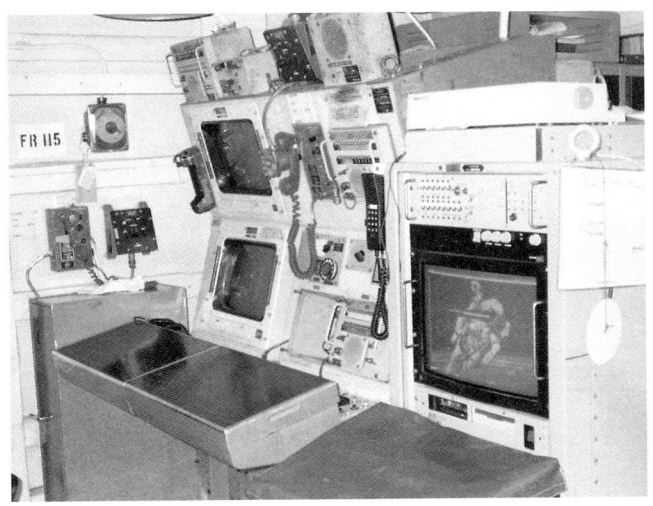

These two photographs were taken in the anti-submarine warfare center aboard the KENNEDY. At left is where the ASW watch officer monitors the tactical picture around the carrier relative to ASW. He is in contact with aircraft and escorting ships. At right is the fast time analyzing system or FTAS. This does just what the name implies by analyzing all data inputs about submarines in the vicinity and the threat they pose to the battle group.

This is Damage Control Central, which is also known as DCC or simply "Central". Here the ship's list is monitored and controlled by moving sea water around in tanks to compensate for the movement of aircraft or from any battle damage. Fire fighting efforts would also be directed from here.

The jet engine maintenance shop is at the aft end of the hangar bay. Here jet engines are inspected and maintained as necessary. They can even be moved out of the shop on to the fantail for test operation if necessary.

This is one of the major propulsion engineering offices, or more simply stated, one of the four engine control rooms. The four engines can produce a total of 280,000 shaft horsepower.

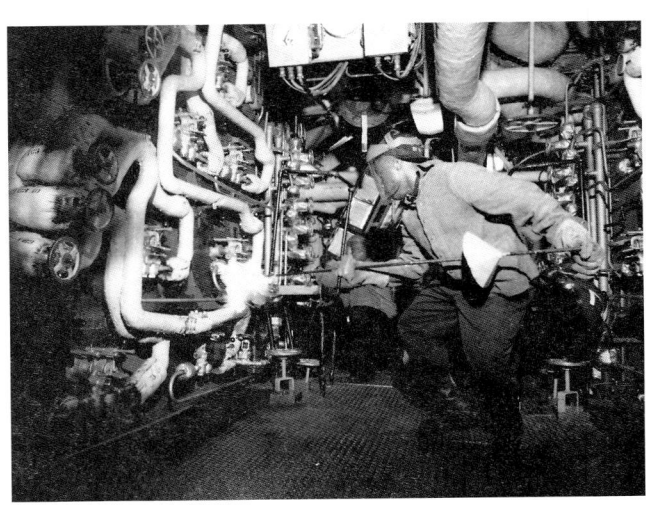

A boiler technician fireman lights one of the boilers in a main engine room. There are two boilers for each engine.

67

This is the captain's inport cabin which is complete with rocking chairs that are exact replicas of President Kennedy's favorite chair. The seating area of the cabin was designed to emulate a room in the Kennedy White House. The carpet is a copy in the color of a White House carpet, and extensive use is made of wood panels and oak decking elsewhere in the cabin.
(National Archives)

The flag cabin is as nice and comfortable as master bedrooms in most modern homes.

The ship's officers usually take their meals in this mess area which is located on the second deck.

Officers assigned to the air wing eat in this officer's mess which is located well forward on the 03 level.

This enlisted mess is on the second deck and is far less formal than the facilities for the officers. Over 15,600 meals are served each day when the ship is at sea with her full crew and air wing.
(National Archives)

Mess personnel are continually preparing meals or snacks. Cheeseburgers are known as "sliders" and if you ever eat one you will know why. The "sliders" that the author has eaten aboard several carriers are the best cheeseburgers he has ever had! They are made with freshly baked bread.
(National Archives)

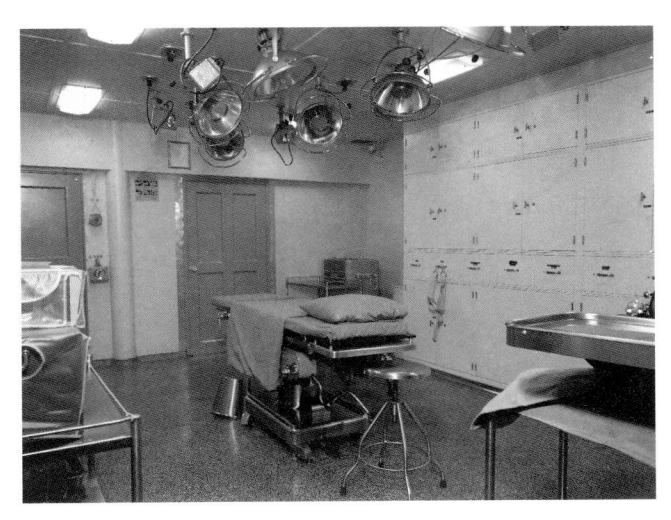

The medical department aboard KENNEDY has facilities equivalent to an eighty-four bed hospital. This is one of the fully equipped operating rooms. (National Archives)

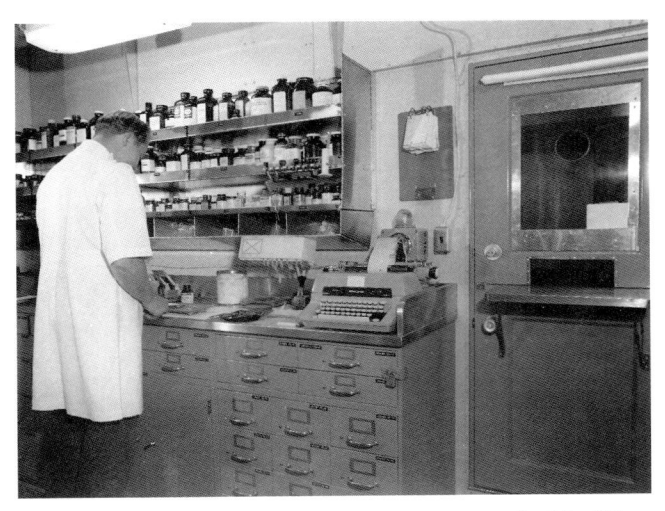

A well stocked pharmacy is also part of the medical facilities aboard the carrier. (National Archives)

When members of the ship's company are off duty, they can visit this well stocked library to increase their knowledge or read for entertainment. (National Archives)

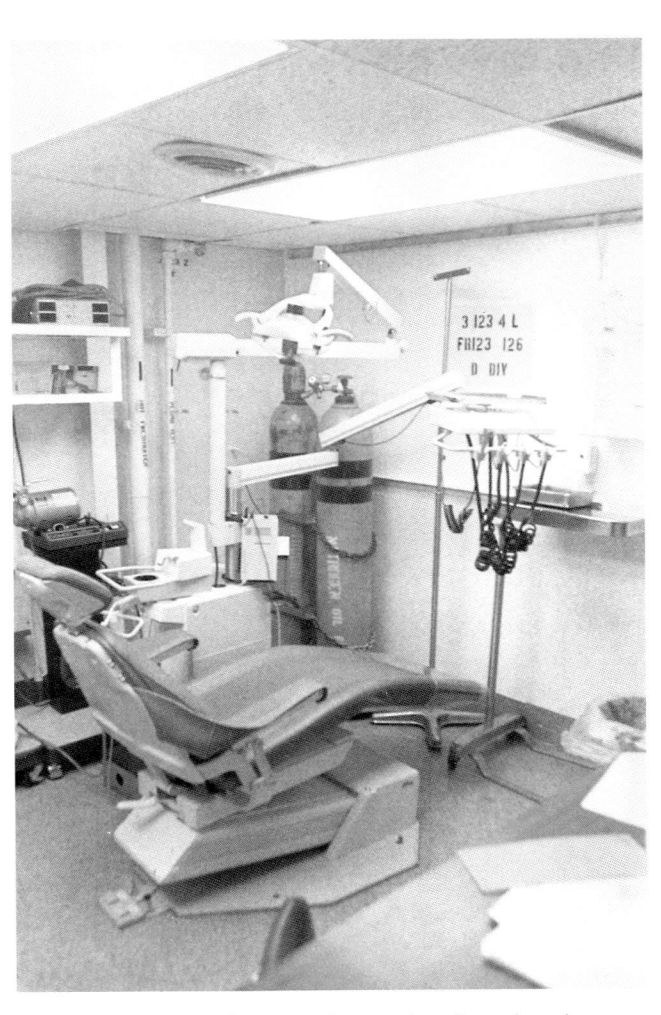

The dental division is as modern and well equipped as any dentist's or oral surgeon's office. This is one of several dental rooms aboard KENNEDY.

A print shop turns out everything from the KENNEDY's own small newspaper to flyers that welcome visitors aboard. (National Archives)

MODELERS SECTION

The Academy/Minicraft kit of the USS JOHN F. KENNEDY is in 1/800th scale and is very similar to the former Monogram kit. It represents the carrier in her early configuration.

There are two model kits of the USS JOHN F. KENNEDY available, and both are in 1/800th scale. The first release was by Monogram, although the kit was not identified as KENNEDY, and the second was by Academy of Korea which is marketed in the United States by Minicraft. The fact is that the Academy/Minicraft kit is almost identical to the Monogram model, but it does have a few minor differences. For example, the stands on which the models are to be displayed are different, and there are some detailing and construction differences as well. The Academy/Minicraft kit has an extra rudder and propeller that indicate that there may have been some thought about motorizing the kit, but there are no other parts provided that would allow this to be done. The words **ON** and **OFF** are molded into the stern (part 3) further indicating that the manufacturer may have intended to offer a motorized version of the kit.

The kits from both manufacturers build up into models that represent KENNEDY's early configuration that remained the same throughout most of the 1970s. Minicraft's instructions claim that the kit is 1/785th scale, and depending on which way you measure it, that could well be true. But it certainly fits into the 1/800th scale collection of carriers offered by Otaki and Arii.

Although Monogram reportedly made different releases of its kit as the KITTY HAWK, the CONSTELLATION, the AMERICA, and the JOHN F. KENNEDY, the only two we have seen are kit number 3007 of the KITTY HAWK, released in 1978, and kit number 3010 of the CONSTELLATION, which was copyrighted in 1987. However, the plastic in these kits represents only the KENNEDY with her unique slanted smokestack and other features. Monogram is not the only company which has failed to learn that it is inaccurate to re-release kits of carriers as other ships simply by changing the numbers on the superstructure and flight deck. Since KENNEDY is a unique one-ship class, and is not part of the KITTY HAWK class as claimed on Minicraft's instruction sheet, a kit of the KENNEDY cannot be built to accurately represent any other carrier.

Most serious scale modelers will not be entirely satisfied with the Monogram or the Academy/Minicraft kits as they come in the box. There are several steps that should be taken that will improve the finished model considerably. In explaining these steps, we will begin with the bottom of the hull and work up. The following comments apply equally to both the Monogram and Academy/Minicraft kits.

The propellers all have four blades and they should have five. We suggest taking correct five-bladed propellers from one of the Arii carrier models in 1/800th scale and using them instead. The propeller shafts have two single supports holding them to the hull. These should be V shaped as illustrated on page 37. They can be corrected by using thin plastic card stock. The fairings where the shafts enter the hull are completely wrong. They were done this way because of mold release considerations. We suggest sanding them off and replacing them with parts from one of the Arii kits. For this we recommend Arii's kit A-123 of the "New" ENTERPRISE.

The original Mk 25 launchers for the BPDMS are included on their sponsons, but these are rather crude box-like affairs that look more like large crates sitting on the deck instead of missile launchers. The modeler should discard these and replace them with ones made from scratch. This is best done by using thin plastic card to make new decks for the sponsons on the ship's quarters and for the swallow's nest on the starboard bow. Then make three Mk 25 launchers from scratch using plastic rod for the pedestal and card stock for the launcher's box. Since the Arii kit of the ENTERPRISE can be built in both her early and late configurations, two Mk 25 launchers are included in that kit, but the modeler will still need a third for KENNEDY.

The railings around the sponsons for the launchers and for the swallow's nest can be replaced with railings from a sheet of photoetched metal. Although there are no photoetched parts in 1/800th scale, it is possible to take a sheet in 1/700th scale and work with that. The thing to do is to take a railing in 1/700th scale that has three rails and cut off the bottom rail. What remains can be used as a railing with two rails in 1/800th scale, and it will look far more realistic than the thick solid plastic railings that come in the kits. The same thing can be done by cutting the bottom rail off of a railing with four rails in 1/700th scale to produce a 1/800th scale railing with three rails. Some modelers will simply be satisfied to use no railings at all in the tiny 1/800th scale. However, we think the model will look much better if the kit railings are replaced with metal ones on the sponsons, swallow's nest, boat decks, and stern. They should also be added to the superstructure. The detailed photographs in this book show where the railings should go.

There are two more changes that must be made to the hull regardless of the time frame the model is being built to represent. First, there is no stem anchor. The hawsepipe is there, but the anchor isn't. The anchor will probably have to be made from scratch since anchors on 1/800th scale models are usually molded as part of the hull. The second addition is the replenishment deck that is located on the structure that supports the

The aft end of the hull and the propeller shafts as they come in the kit are shown at left. Note the inaccurate fairings where the propeller shafts enter the hull and the single supports for the propeller shafts. At right are the corrected hull and the propeller shafts with their V-shaped braces.

Both of the kits of the KENNEDY represent the carrier in her early configuration. To build a model of the ship as she appears today, a lot of updating will have to be done. This photograph shows the port side with sponsons added to the bow and the quarter. Also note how the hangar deck was added using plastic card. In the small 1/800th scale, the hangar deck does not have to be elaborate. Adding the deck shown here took only about two hours of work, but it will add a lot to the finished model. The most difficult part was making the inner walls with the oval openings for the elevators.

starboard overhang and superstructure. It is just aft of the number two elevator, and is illustrated on page 44. This must be added from plastic card, and the appropriate holes must be cut into the side of the ship. This deck has been on the KENNEDY since the ship first put to sea.

We also recommend adding a hangar deck to the carrier. This can be made from plastic card, and does not have to be too elaborate in this small scale. The kits only provide oval shaped openings to the hangar bays that are either closed off with doors or that go back into the hull a short distance. But if a hangar deck is added, the walls with the inner oval openings must also be included.

The flight deck will need a lot of work too. First, the catapults stand far too proud from the deck. Sand them flush with the deck, then rescribe them. Correct the shapes of the JBDs behind cats one, two, and three in the process. The one behind cat four is all right. The landing lines are scribed into the deck. Sand these off and paint the lines on without these molded guides. There is a fifth arresting cable shown, and it is the one associated with the crash barrier. It would not be in place unless the crash barrier was rigged, so it too must be sanded away. It is the fourth cable forward from the rear of the deck. The platform for the fresnel lens is provided, but the lens isn't. One should be added from plastic card and sprue. The LSO platform must also be added. The netting for it is present, but the platform itself isn't. Other details, such as the whip antennas, which can be made from stretched sprue, should be added to the flight deck as the modeler desires. If a post-1990 KENNEDY is being modeled, the catapult overrun for cat two should be removed. This means that netting should replace it, and this might have to come from another kit. Also for a present day KENNEDY, the modeler can have hours of fun cutting 333 self-inflating life rafts from thin plastic rod. We found that .035-inch rod seemed to be the right diameter. Gluing these to the catwalks around the flight deck may require a reservation in the psycho ward!

The superstructure is fairly accurate for the original configuration, and the lattice radar mast is about as good as can be done with molded plastic. Five F-4 Phantoms, seven A-4 Skyhawks, and three A-3 Skywarriors are included, and these can and should be supplemented with aircraft from other 1/800th scale kits.

Building either the Monogram or the Academy/Minicraft kit to represent KENNEDY as she appears today will take a considerable amount of work. New sponsons will have to be built from scratch for the two quarters to support the Mk 29 Sea Sparrow launchers and their associated radars. Another sponson will have to be added to the port bow for the Phalanx mount, and other Phalanx systems must be added to the side of the superstructure and to the port quarter. Additions must be made to the superstructure, and the radar fit must be changed. Again, many of the required parts like the Mk 29 launchers, the Mk 78 radars, and the AN/SPS-49 radar can be found in Arii's kit A-123 of the ENTERPRISE. However, this kit provides only three Mk 78 radars. Therefore the rest must be made from scratch or taken from yet another kit.

The best thing the modeler can do in building a model of KENNEDY as she appears today is to consider the kit as merely the basic form with which he has to work. He should then study each section of this book that illustrates the ship's details. Using plastic card, rod, and sprue, and by cannibalizing parts from other 1/800th scale carrier kits, the modeler can then detail each part of the ship as shown in the photographs.

To build the sponsons on the quarters, we used plastic card, but wood worked better for the sponson on the port bow that mounts the Phalanx gun system. Its unusual shape with compound curves would be hard to make out of card stock, but it is

This photograph shows an update, a correction, and an improvement to the starboard side. The sponsons for the Mark 29 Sea Sparrow launcher and its associated radars have been added to the quarter. The replenishment deck that is under the overhang support is missing from the kit and has been added from plastic card. The deck with the Mark 25 missile launcher that is provided in the kit for the swallow's nest has been replaced with a piece of plastic card. A Mark 29 launcher and railings will be added later during the model's construction.

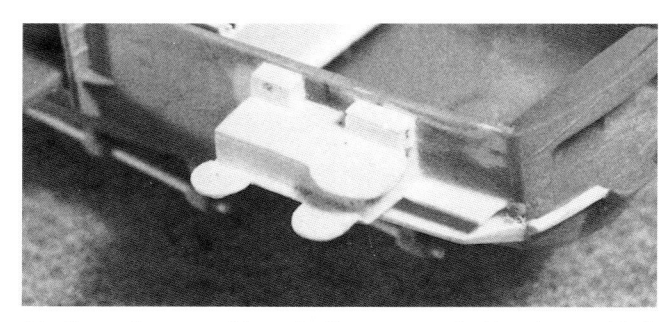

Plastic card was used to make the sponson that has been added to the port quarter. Although it is provided in the kit, the small deck below the sponson has also been made from plastic card, and a small addition to the stern can also be seen in this close-up view. Once the additions have been filled, sanded, primed, and sanded again, the railings, Mark 29 Sea Sparrow launcher, radars, and Phalanx gun system will be added to complete this update to the model.

The modifications and additions made to the starboard quarter are shown here. In this case all construction was done with plastic card.

The sponson for the Phalanx mount on the port bow was carved from pine. Because of its compound curves, it was easier to use wood for this update rather than to make it from plastic card. After it is primed and sanded, the sponson will be ready for the addition of the railings and the Phalanx mount. Other smaller details will also be added.

The replenishment deck under the starboard overhang is not provided in the kits, but it has been on KENNEDY since she first put to sea. This was constructed using plastic card, and the four holes in the side of the carrier were drilled out. Once this addition is filled, sanded, and primed, small details and the railings will be added.

rather simple to carve out of a small piece of pine. Plastic card was used to make the missing replenishment deck just aft of elevator number two.

To update and improve the flight deck, we sanded it smooth except for the four arresting cables. We then rescribed the catapults, JBDs, and armament elevators. The catapult overrun for cat two was removed, and we also removed all of the plastic safety netting between the port side and the remaining overrun. A single piece of plastic netting that was cut from another kit was then glued on to the bow. This replaced not only the netting we removed, but it covered in the gap left by removing the port side overrun. Stretched sprue was used to make the whip antennas that would be added around the flight deck, as illustrated in the various photographs in this book.

Using plastic card stock, we added the Phalanx deck and other new details to the starboard side of the superstructure. The three Phalanx mounts and Mk 78 radars came from two Arii ENTERPRISE kits, as did the Mk 29 Sea Sparrow launchers. The SPS-49 radar antenna was taken from an Arii ENTERPRISE kit, but it required the addition of a scratchbuilt feed horn. Both the azimuth and elevation domes for the SPN-41 automatic landing control radar had to be made from scratch.

Aircraft were taken from other 1/800th scale carrier kits to represent the types in KENNEDY's air wing during Operation Desert Storm. While most of these went on the flight deck and elevators, a few were reserved to go on the scratchbuilt hangar deck.

The Academy/Minicraft kit provides decals for the KENNEDY, and they are all right if the ship in her pre-1980 configuration is being modeled. However, if the model is being built to represent the carrier as she appears today, the modeler will have to paint the outlined **67** on the flight deck and use other decals for the **67** on the starboard side of the smokestack. This **67** should be shaded in black, but the decals in the kit are not. One of the **67**s in the kit can be used on the port side of the superstructure. The kit decal sheet also does not provide the ship's name for the stern.

The landing lines are easily painted on the deck, but the foul lines and the markings around the elevators are a different story. We used Scalemaster's stripes for this purpose. We took the thinnest white stripe that they provide, then painted alternating red segments across it using a small brush. We then used a clear straight edge and cut the decal film and excess red paint away from each side by running our razor knife right down the edge of the white decal. This provided the decals for the foul lines. The markings around the elevators were made the same way by painting red segments on thin yellow decal stripes. This is a bit tedious, but it will result in excellent markings for the flight deck. When the decal stripe is dipped in water, the excess film and red paint can be discarded, and all that is left is the white or yellow stripe with alternating red segments.

In 1/800th scale many of the smaller radar antennas, search lights, and other small details are just too tiny to reproduce. Just how far to go is up to the desires and talents of the individual modeler. But the detailed photographs included in this book should provide sufficient reference material for a modeler to spend hundreds of hours making these small parts from scratch. The Monogram and Academy/Minicraft kits may be small and lacking in detail, but a very attractive and accurate model can result if the builder is willing to put in the time and effort. Press time for this book arrived before we completed our model, but we are looking forward to finishing it in the future.